THE FRIENDSHIP BOOK

of

Francis Gay

☆

A THOUGHT
FOR EACH DAY
IN 1961

D. C. THOMSON & CO., LTD. JOHN LENG & CO., LTD.
LONDON - GLASGOW - MANCHESTER - DUNDEE

We live in deeds not years, in thoughts not breaths;
In feelings, not in figures on a dial.
We should count time by heart throbs. He most lives
Who thinks most - feels the noblest - acts the best.

Philip James Bailey.

JANUARY

SUNDAY—JANUARY 1.

THE Lord bless thee, and keep thee: the Lord make His face to shine upon thee, and be gracious unto thee: the Lord lift up His countenance upon thee, and give thee peace.

MONDAY—JANUARY 2.

ON the first Sunday of the year, when an elder on duty at the door of Wishart Memorial Church, Dundee, arrived at the kirk, he found two half-crowns lying on a table in the vestibule.

No name, no indication who they were from. Just two half-crowns, gifts from the first arrivals—" the Church's first-foot," as the elder put it.

Rather a fine gesture, wasn't it?

TUESDAY—JANUARY 3.

DON'T get rattled if you've a biggish job waiting to be begun. Keep your head. Take your time. Go easy.

I say this because of what a schoolboy said to me the other day.

He's brilliant. He has already passed his Ordinary Level G.C.E. in eight subjects ; and though so very young he is now specialising in only three subjects : Mathematics, Higher Mathematics and Physics.

" But tell me, Duncan," I said, trying not to let him guess how envious I was of his prowess, " won't you find higher maths frightfully difficult?"

Said the boy : " Oh, I don't think so. You see, it's really only like learning your two-times table in the infant school . . . you learn one thing one day and something else the next, and it soon piles up !"

WEDNESDAY—JANUARY 4.

BRAVE the rough, enjoy the smooth
As you plod along,
Thank your stars for what is right—
Never mind the wrong.
All life's ills and cares forget—
Keep in mind, instead,
Any pleasant, happy things
Friendly people said.
And if troubles come your way,
Do not use a gun . . .
How could there be shadows if
Never shone the sun?

THURSDAY—JANUARY 5.

AS I walked down the garden path the other morning I saw a little gentleman in a greenish-brown suit. He sported a bright red waistcoat, and looked plump and prosperous. It may surprise you if I add that he was actually sitting on my garden wall.

Yes, there on the wall he was, looking as if he had no end of time to spare. I cannot say he was singing, but every so often he gave a shrill, merry call, and he kept his head cocked as he watched me with one black and beady eye.

I confess that he did not speak my language, and I may possibly have misunderstood him, but I am pretty sure he was saying to me: "I'll grin and bear it a bit longer. This weather can't last for ever, you know. No point in grousing about things, really—and if I make a fuss because it's chilly now I'll soon be complaining that there's not a cool spot anywhere except in the shade of the old apple tree!"

So I nodded and grinned. I raised my hat to the robin on my wall . . . and set off for the office determined to smile my way into spring.

FRIDAY—JANUARY 6.

JUST because a minister hasn't become a TV personality or isn't a pulpit orator doesn't mean he fails to bless and comfort many.

Just because a man isn't outstandingly successful in business isn't proof that he isn't giving all he can give to his job.

Just because a university student fails to run off with the highest honours can never be taken to indicate that in years to come he will be a failure. . . .

It isn't so much what we do that counts as what we try to do. After all, most of us are very ordinary folk—but what a lot of good we can do and how wonderfully we can bless others if only we do our best!

SATURDAY—JANUARY 7.

YES, if you saw the work of Mrs Jeffrey's hands you would be lost in admiration.

She can darn with silk and nylon and wool so beautifully that I would defy you to spot the repair.

And you would never guess how it all began.

Mrs Jeffrey was only five when she was struck by serious trouble in her leg. It was then that she darned her first pair of socks.

She sat up in bed, a wee girl working with all the patience of womanhood. And with love, too, for with twelve brothers and sisters running about, her mother needed her help.

As time went on, her fingers grew long and sensitive and agile. Even when she hurried her darning, her touch was cool and steady. And the wonderful thing is that the gift she found in her three years in bed has never left her.

Isn't it a splendid thing that an infirmity of many years ago should bring with it a blessing that has lasted a lifetime?

SUNDAY—JANUARY 8.

AND the blind and the lame came to Him in the temple; and He healed them.

MONDAY—JANUARY 9.

I THINK these words of John Ruskin's are worth considering :—

The essence of lying is in deception, not in words. A lie may be told by silence, by equivocation, by accent on a syllable, by a glance of the eye attaching a peculiar significance to a sentence; and all these kinds of lies are worse and baser by many degrees than a lie plainly worded.

TUESDAY—JANUARY 10.

QUEEN VICTORIA had her breakfast in a waiting-room at Perth Station . . . King Edward VII popped off the train to buy a walking stick for his collection . . .

Oh, yes, the highest in the land have come Perth's way and still do. But I'll not be thinking of them when next I visit there. I'll be looking for leading mail porter Albert McMillan.

Albert works among the Post Office vans at the north end of the station. It's a cold job, especially at five o'clock in the morning.

But Albert and his mates brought Perth Station a new honour. They won a £50 first prize for having the best-kept main line station in Scotland.

It was the first time Perth had won and it meant an extra 10s out of the blue to Albert as his share.

He got the money just when it seemed he'd need it because of a threatened strike. Yet, do you know what he did with it? He promptly sent it to me to help others! Thank you, Albert.

WEDNESDAY—JANUARY 11.

A LETTER from " down under " says,
" Dear Francis, It is hot!"
It makes me wonder what they've done
To have what we've not got.

But wait—life's fair enough, no doubt,
When winter howls " below,"
We'll sit in sunshine, eat ice cream,
And watch our marrows grow!

THURSDAY—JANUARY 12.

THE Rev. James Wood was visiting a hospital to give Communion to two old ladies who lay side by side.

As it happened, another old lady was visiting them, so Mr Wood invited her to join in the service.

At first she hesitated. Then she explained she was very deaf, and wouldn't hear the words. " Never mind," Mr Wood said. " I'll speak the service into your ear."

So it was.

Gently but clearly, Mr Wood went through the service, word by word, while the deaf woman sat close beside him.

When he came to the injunction—" This do in remembrance of Me." she turned to him, and to his surprise he saw her eyes filled with tears.

" Mr Wood," she said, " that's the first time I've heard these words for 30 years."

It was only then the minister realised that though the woman had been going along to her kirk, she had never been able to hear what the minister was saying and so had missed the very heart of the Sacrament.

Only six words, yet they meant so much to a deaf old woman.

FRIDAY—JANUARY 13.

A FRIEND who lives in California sends me these lines to remember in the coming year.

To help another on life's way,
To smile and chase a frown away,
To hide a fault, reveal the good,
To love my neighbours as I should,
To bring good cheer to one who's sad,
To make a lonely body glad,
To share my joys—and blessings, too—
This will I try each day to do!

SATURDAY—JANUARY 14.

I FOR one will always bless the day Archie Read took a pain in his shoulder!

If you think that's a strange thing for Francis Gay to say—read on, and I'm sure you'll agree with me.

Mr Read felt the pain in 1926. He was an electrical engineer, and he made a little pad through which he threaded cotton-covered wire. Then he plugged it into electricity and laid it against his aching shoulder and neck. Like magic, the warm pad soothed the pains away.

Next, Mr Read made a bigger heated pad and fitted it to his bed. Yes—the first electric blanket!

It worked so well he made another, for the spare room. When a doctor friend came to stay, and sampled the comfort of the electric blanket, he asked Mr Read to make three more for him.

Now a million electric blankets are made by firms in Britain every year.

So now you know why, as I slip into my cosy bed on these cold winter nights, I always bless that pain in Archie Read's shoulder. And I'm sure that if you've ever experienced the bliss of an electric blanket, you'll do the same!

SUNDAY—JANUARY 15.

EXCEPT the Lord build the house, they labour in vain that build it.

MONDAY—JANUARY 16.

NEXT time you pass down the street, look about you at the windows and doors, and ponder over what I have to say.

Recently members of one city church have visited every home in their parish. They are ordinary folk like you and me—students, teachers, bakers, housewives, labourers, typists, professional men and apprentices of all ages.

What, you may ask, have they been finding behind these doors? In most cases happy, well-cared-for families. But in far too many others they have found despair and utter loneliness.

In one home they came upon a family sitting in the guttering light of a few tuppenny candles . . . for the husband was out of work, the mother was due to go into hospital, there was no money to pay the gas bills . . . so there they sat in the gloom, wondering where to turn.

In another home there was no light at all. An old man lived there alone, friendless and hopeless. His wife was dead, his two sons had been killed in the war. He just sat in his chair all day, and when darkness fell he went to bed, for there was nothing else to do or see—no purpose to his existence.

Why, some of the girls of the church came back in tears at the things they'd seen.

It may seem strange that these things can happen in times when so much is done for the needy. But if they can happen within sight of a living kirk like this, God knows the challenge that human need presents to us all in our own surroundings.

TUESDAY—JANUARY 17.

JOHN DUNCAN, born in 1794 at Stonehaven, was a remarkable man.

No one knew more about poverty than he did. He never went to school and as a herd boy he was cruelly ill-treated—and was shy ever after.

Eventually, he became a weaver and lived in a loft at Auchleven.

He made one set of clothes last half a hundred years and spent no more than four shillings a week on bed, board and laundry.

Honest as the day, hard working, humble in spirit, he enjoyed life to within his last few months, dying at 87.

Flowers meant everything to him. He used to say that as a laddie, " I just took a notion to know one plant by another when I was running about the hills. And as I had a good memory, when I knew a flower once I knew it always."

So the wild flower man, who was as poor as a church mouse, held up his head, talked with rich and poor about his precious flowers and, though he never went to school, managed to teach himself Latin and Greek and grammer and botany and science . . . every day discovering some bit of knowledge he had not known before, and thus all his days he was adventuring.

Somehow, as I read about old John, who had so little, yet enjoyed life so much, I found myself asking whether I was making the best of my life.

WEDNESDAY—JANUARY 18.

NOW, if you say you'll do a thing,
Don't shout ere it's begun ;
Leave shouting to the folk who see
What you attempted DONE !

THURSDAY—JANUARY 19.

EVERY now and again most women get sick of the sight of their kitchen and feel like running away to the south of France or Hollywood or somewhere. Who can wonder at this? Who can blame them? Isn't it routine that just about breaks the strongest will?

But most women, feeling that way, give themselves a shake or may be a wee treat (tea and toast at a cafe) and go back to the daily round thankful they've a man and some children to care for!

It all sounds stupid, of course . . . but that's the way it is, isn't it?

FRIDAY—JANUARY 20.

JUST after the war Rev. J. Ford McLeod visited wee Jimmy McGowan in hospital. Jimmy, although bedridden for five years, was tremendously keen on cricket.

The minister sent Jimmy's autograph book to Denis Compton, asking if he could have the signatures of the English and South African Test players.

You can imagine how excited the wee boy was as every post arrived—wondering if his prized book would come back. But as the days lengthened into weeks, and still no book arrived, Jimmy's excitement turned to disappointment.

Then one afternoon about two months later, Jimmy handed the minister a letter he'd received that morning from Denis Compton himself.

In it, the cricketer apologised to Jimmy for the delay in returning his book, but explained he'd had to send it to South Africa as some of the team had gone home before they'd added their signatures!

Nothing makes me feel better than to see the great sparing a thought for the small!

SATURDAY—JANUARY 21.

I PASS on these thoughts about this life of ours:—

Life is like driving with one's back to the horses —one never sees the good things till they are passed. (*Lord Gorell.*)

It will never rain roses. If you want more roses you must plant more trees. (*George Eliot.*)

Everyone's a failure at some time of their lives. The thing is to see that it isn't chronic. (*Susan Ertz.*)

Nature has given us life at interest like money, with no day fixed for repayment. (*Cicero.*)

SUNDAY—JANUARY 22.

WOE be unto the pastors that destroy and scatter the sheep of My pasture! saith the Lord.

MONDAY—JANUARY 23.

EDITH RAE had lived in a wee cottage in Angus, and although it was only on special occasions that she managed far beyond her garden gate, her influence went out infinitely farther.

She had never been blessed with good health, yet she had a knack of listening to other folk's worries and making them seem easier to bear.

She nursed her old mother faithfully until the old body passed on just after her hundredth birthday.

I don't know if it was the strain of this that did it—but just afterwards Edith had to go into hospital and there she passed quietly away.

What was her secret? Simply this. Everybody's troubles were her troubles—and in helping with the problems of other folk, she found no time to worry about herself.

Tuesday—January 24.

EVEN to look at Sir Malcolm Sargent makes you think everything is bound to go his way. Can you think of anyone who seems more gay and imperturbable . . . a man who seems to have none of the worries and cares of the rest of us?

How mistaken you would be, for Sir Malcolm has had perhaps more heartbreak than many of us.

In 1933, when his future as a conductor was beginning to be assured, he was struck down with tuberculosis. He lay gravely ill and wasn't expected to live. But for two years he fought back, in and out of hospital, and gradually recovered his health.

Just when the way seemed clear ahead, tragedy struck again. This time, his little daughter Pamela fell a victim to polio. For seven years she lay crippled, while her father poured into his music all the heartbreak he suffered and the hope he cherished. Alas, Pamela never recovered.

Despite all that, Sir Malcolm believes there are things we can understand only through suffering or affliction. His secret lies in the three qualities which he himself possesses, and tries to live by.

First there's kindliness and neighbourliness. Second a sense of humour—and third, as he himself puts it, the gift of a good Christian faith. For to people who have faith there is surely nothing in the world that can touch them.

Wednesday—January 25.

IT'S grand to have a windfall,
That's sure to set you singing.
It's grand to get promotion
Or see your own team winning.
But, oh! there's nothing thrills you so
As does the joy of GIVING!

Thursday—January 26.

A VISIT to the local library or bookshop, to browse through shelves and shelves of books; to read again the classics, or the works of a brilliant new author; to delve into the history of great nations, or the biographies of great men and women; to travel by means of the printed page into foreign lands; to turn again to the greatest of all books, the Bible. No one need ever be lonely with all these many friends around. For books are friends.

Oliver Goldsmith made this point best when he wrote, "The first time I read an excellent book, it is to me just as if I had gained a new friend. When I read over a book I have perused before, it resembles the meeting with an old one."

Friday—January 27.

ONE evening a minister called on an old man who had come through a serious operation and was now at home convalescing.

They chatted away for a while, and then the minister stood up. "I'll have to go now," he said. "I want to see two of your friends in the infirmary who are going through their operations soon."

The old man caught the minister's sleeve. "Would you take a message to them?" he asked

"Of course," was the reply. "What do you want me to tell them?"

"Just say that Isaiah 41, Verse 10, will help them as much as it helped me."

"Fear thou not: for I am with thee; be not dismayed; for I am thy God. I will strengthen thee, yea, I will help thee . . . I will uphold thee with the right hand of my righteousness."

The old man sent his friends the most valuable of all his possessions—a little of his own shining faith.

SATURDAY—JANUARY 28.

THE Lady of the House has recently acquired an antique willow pattern plate. She is delighted with it, and I think it will be on show for many a year.

You'll know the legend of the willow pattern plate, of course—it is more than 2000 years old, and it's about a lovely Chinese maiden who loved and was loved by one of her father's servants. The girl's name was Knoon-shee, and that of her lover was Chang.

But as you'll remember Knoon-shee's father planned for his daughter to marry a wealthy suitor. When the maiden refused, her angry father locked her in a little house in the garden—we can see the house to the left of the temple on our willow pattern plate. Somehow she managed to send a message to Chang: "Gather thy blossom ere it be stolen!"

Along came the gallant lover, rescued the maiden and carried her across the little three-arch bridge while the father threatened as he brandished a whip. The lovers were fortunate enough to escape by means of a little ship (shown on the plate) and lived on an island of dreams till the wicked father and the wealthy suitor found their hiding place and set the house on fire one night while the lovers slept.

It's an old, old story, and a sad, sad story . . . until you look up and see flying above the gardens and the trees and the flowers and the ship and the temple and the quaint fences and the pretty flowers—two doves in the blue and cloudless sky . . . the spirits, the immortal spirits of Knoon-shee and Chang, eternally happy.

SUNDAY—JANUARY 29.

LOVE not the world, neither the things that are in the world. If any man love the world, the love of the Father is not in him.

MONDAY—JANUARY 30.

A TOURIST in Scotland came to a small loch, and asked an old Scotsman to row him across.

The old man readily agreed, and the tourist soon found himself nearing the farther shore. Then he noticed that on one oar the boatman had carved the word "Faith," and on the other the word "Works."

"What's the idea?" he asked.

"I'll show you," replied the old man. Straightaway he dropped one of the oars and began plying the one called Faith. As a result, the boat moved in a circle.

Then the boatman dropped that oar and began plying the one named Works. Instantly the boat began going round and round in the opposite direction.

Lastly, with a smile on his wrinkled face, the boatman pulled steadily at both oars. "We're getting somewhere now," he declared.

And perhaps that's as good a summary of practical religion as we'll ever come across.

TUESDAY—JANUARY 31.

A FAMILY man is one who has replaced the pound notes in his wallet with photographs.

You can't change the past, but you can ruin a perfectly happy present by worrying too much about the future.

Most folk wouldn't get to the top if the going were easy.

A wise bride is one who loses her temper permanently.

Happy people are those who know how to be tough with themselves and tender with others.

A dour member of the kirk, when asked by his minister for a donation, replied—"This Christian business is nothing but give, give, give." Replied the minister—"You're right—Christians do *just* that."

IN PRAISE OF THE COBBLER

Praise we the cobbler's art—
Shoes that are sturdy and neat.
For we'd all of us be in the cart
If he didn't keep us on our feet!

David Hope

A HIGHLAND BURN

The Lord in wisdom took
Water and rocks in turn,
And borrowed from the thunder peal
To make a mountain burn.

DAVID HOPE

FEBRUARY

Wednesday—February 1.

LET cold winds blow, come rain or snow
When winter nights are dark,
And storms arise, and moonless skies
Of starlight have no spark.
Then happy is the man whose wife
Can by the fire sit,
And smile at him, and be content
To chat awhile or knit.
Though storms to threaten us begin,
Who cares, if all is peace within?

Thursday—February 2.

IF you happened to walk down a quiet road off Kensington High Street, London, you might pass the little shop without noticing it.

Yet that shop means more than words can say to Jean Harvey—and hundreds like her.

Jean was only 22 when she was stricken by polio. But she fought back with patience and faith until she could walk again—on crutches.

What future, you might wonder, was there now for a girl left crippled like Jean? Well, it seemed God had a purpose after all, for it was in hospital that she found her life's work. She discovered many disabled folk like herself had to sit at home seemingly no use to themselves or to others.

Jean felt sure she could help, so she put her savings into a small shop and contacted other disabled people. They for their part made things at home and sent them for her to sell for them.

Isn't this another example of what might have been the end—but what turned out to be a splendid new beginning?

FRIDAY—FEBRUARY 3.

WHILE a minister was rummaging through a desk the other day, he came across something that brought back memories of one of the richest women he has ever known.

She was a member of his congregation and, although she was rich, she had scarcely a penny to her name when she died, for her riches were of the spirit.

It was while he was going through her belongings that he found a cutting pasted to a framed photograph of her in her younger days. On the paper was a verse—"A Priceless Gift"—which apparently had been the secret of her attitude to life:—

"To your enemy, forgiveness; to a customer, service; to an opponent, tolerance; to a friend, your heart; to a child, a good example; to yourself, respect; to all men, charity; to God, what belongs to Him."

SATURDAY—FEBRUARY 4.

CAN you imagine how Lora Bell felt?

Lora was standing alone in the crowded balcony of a strange church. There was just one seat vacant, right at the end of the front row.

What if she went forward and found it was being kept for someone? What would she do?

Maybe Lora was beginning to wish she hadn't gone to the church to hear her girl-friend sing in the choir.

But shyly she went forward and asked the man sitting next to the vacant seat if he was keeping it for someone.

The man smiled. "Yes," he said—and Lora's spirits sank. Then he added—"Yes, I'm keeping it for YOU!"

That's the kind of welcome I like to hear strangers getting at the kirk.

SUNDAY—FEBRUARY 5.

JESUS answered them and said, My doctrine is not Mine, but His that sent Me.

MONDAY—FEBRUARY 6.

IN Sunday school, wee Brian was asked whether Solomon was a rich man or a poor man.

"A poor man," he replied.

"How do you make that out?" asked his teacher.

"Well," said Brian, "it says in first Kings that Solomon slept with his fathers. I think if he had been a rich man he would have slept on his own."

TUESDAY—FEBRUARY 7.

"BY cool Siloam's shady rill, how sweet the lily grows." How the melody of those beautiful words lifts us far away on wondrous wings!

Reginald Heber wrote them. He was a parson from near Crewe, who faithfully visited his flock, taking all kinds of risks to comfort the stricken.

One Saturday afternoon he dashed off three verses of a new hymn for his father-in-law. The older man was delighted, but not Heber. So he wrote a fourth verse beginning, "Waft, waft, ye winds," and the hymn we know today—"From Greenland's Icy Mountains"—was given to the world.

He also wrote "Holy, Holy, Holy, Lord God Almighty" and "Brightest And Best Of The Sons Of The Morning" and into them all went some of the grace and melody of his own happy faith.

There were those who frowned on Heber's happy hymns, but they are long gone. The music is still with us after more than 130 years, and I mean no disrespect when I recommend on these dull days a good dose of Heber's tonic!

Wednesday—February 8.

SURE, times there are when I could weep—
So many troubles mine,
So much that irks or hurts or grieves
About which I could whine.

But times there are when suddenly
My wealth of joy seems vast;
I count my blessings—every one
More precious than the last.

Thursday—February 9.

A FRIEND writes to say that in Hollister, a small town in California, lives a shoemaker called Bruno.

Everybody thereabouts tells everybody else to take their shoes to Bruno because he gives a free shine, a pair of new laces and a lot of help.

Not long ago, a visitor walked into Bruno's shop and said—" People say such things about you, Mr Bruno, that I'm sure you are a man who prays. Is that so?"

" Sure. But mostly I pray for the other fellow."

" What other fellow?" asked the visitor.

" Well, everybody . . . and that means you and the people outside my window at this minute."

" And praying for others helps you?"

" Sure. And it makes everybody a bit happier. It means that all people are my friends because I pray for their happiness. A man, say, comes into the shop. I ask God to make him happier, and to tell me how to speak to him to bless him."

" And you make good money?"

" Sure, and who can ever do without money . . . but happiness, that is more important. Kindness—that is best."

FRIDAY—FEBRUARY 10.

WE don't hear much about him now, but at one time Emile Coué was known to everybody.

That was forty years ago when people, at this time of the year, were as likely to have coughs and colds and aches and pains as they are now.

Emile was a doctor, and what he said to his patients is worth remembering. When they moaned in his surgery he told them to hurry off home, take his prescription, and say to themselves: "Every day, in every way, I'm getting better and better!"

It worked!

SATURDAY—FEBRUARY 11.

BLESSED are the givers . . . especially the prompt ones. Like old Mary.

Mary was one of the first to take home a collecting box for her self-denial offerings for the Salvation Army. In no time at all, it seemed, she brought it back almost full.

How she managed it, I don't know, but nothing would do but she would take away another box.

Then the weather began to tell on the old soul, and she worried in case the second box wouldn't be full in time. So she coaxed the doctor, coalman and insurance man to put in a little something to hurry on the good work. Then she handed in the offering.

They were surprised to see her back so soon. But there she was, explaining that she wanted to make sure her box was in as she might not be well enough to bring it to the self-denial gift service—in March!

It says on the lid of the little box, "Give unto the Lord the glory due unto His name: bring an offering and come into His courts."

I can't help feeling that it's already noted in the Great Book that old Mary came four weeks early.

SUNDAY—FEBRUARY 12.

AND I give unto them eternal life; and tney shall never perish, neither shall any man pluck them out of My hand.

MONDAY—FEBRUARY 13.

WHEN things perplex you, and the way ahead is darkened by doubt and fear, try to remember Christopher Columbus!

You see, when Columbus set out on his voyage of discovery, he didn't know *where he was going.*

When he arrived on the strange shores of America, he didn't know *where he was.*

When he got back, he didn't even know *where he'd been.*

And yet he knew beyond a shadow of a doubt that he had found a great, new world.

TUESDAY—FEBRUARY 14.

THE Lady of the House laughed when I told her this story about a four-year-old boy who'd just had a visit from his granny.

"Daddy," said the boy, "I do like Grandma, don't you?"

"Of course I do," smiled his father. "She's my mother."

The boy thought for a moment, his brow furrowed. "Oh," he murmured, "I didn't know that." Then he added, "But when I grow up I'm going to marry Gran, I like her so much."

His father smiled again. "Son," he protested gently, "you can't marry my mother, surely?"

Again the wee boy frowned—but like magic his face cleared. "Why not?" he asked triumphantly. "*You* married *my* mother, didn't you?"

WEDNESDAY—FEBRUARY 15.

IT takes very little to help folk along—
A word may bring comfort in grief,
A smile or some help to the harassed or worn
Can cheer a hard day past belief.
It takes very little—but have we the wit
To see where it's needed a lot,
The heart quick to share, and the hand which is there,
And ready to give what we've got?

THURSDAY—FEBRUARY 16.

WHETHER or not today's teenagers are familiar with the name Patti I couldn't say, but to older folk it still conjures up those far-off years when Madame Adelina Patti was the greatest soprano in the world.

Adelina was on her honeymoon at Cannes. She had arranged for letters to be sent on to her, so one morning she walked in to the post office and asked for her letters. "What name?" inquired the official, looking over the counter.

"Baroness Adelina de Cederstrom-Patti," was the reply.

Quite properly, the official asked—"You must prove it. Have you, for example, an old letter you can show me?"

Adelina hadn't. So there was the world-famous singer trying in vain to prove she was who she said she was.

Suddenly she had an idea. Without stirring from the counter, she began singing . . . singing as only Madame Patti could sing, in that glorious voice which seemed to fall from the stars. Folk in the post office and folk outside listened with rapture . . . and when the song was ended, the little post office official handed over the letters with a bow!

FRIDAY—FEBRUARY 17.

THIS new day is a challenge to you.

You can waste it, allowing its precious hours to pass without doing anything worthwhile. That's a poor way of using the minutes between waking and sleeping.

Or you can use it to some purpose—you can thank God for what is good; you can learn something or begin a big task or finish a long-delayed piece of work. You can sing. You can help somebody. You can cheer a friend and share a neighbour's burden. You can forgive. You can go the second mile. You can look for the best and do your best and *be* your best . . . and go to bed feeling that you have put into this day and got out of it as much as you possibly could.

SATURDAY—FEBRUARY 18.

THE next time you're inclined to feel sorry for yourself at having to lie in bed with a cold or flu, think of Mary Jean in the Shetlands. For almost sixty years she has been confined to bed.

When Queen Victoria was on the throne, and the Boer War had just begun, Mary Jean was a fresh-faced lassie knowing the joys of being sweet 16. Then one day, while crossing a field, she fell.

Soon she couldn't walk without stumbling, and eventually, doctors gave the grim verdict that there was nothing more they could do for her.

So at 24, just when a young woman should be setting up a house of her own—Mary Jean knew she'd never leave her bed again.

Yet after all these years, no one has ever heard her complain.

Blessings on you, Mary Jean! You're an inspiration to us all.

HOLIDAYS

Remember those days at the seaside?
Waves coming rows upon rows,
Little fish left in a pool by the tide
And the feel of the sand in your toes?

B

DAVID HOPE

TRACKS IN THE SNOW

We all leave tracks
Wherever we go,
In our lives
As in the snow.

So I must live
That, following mine,
Folk pass from shadow
To sunshine.

DAVID HOPE

AN OLD CASTLE

Where are the warriors now?
The clansmen of old?
Gone like snow from the hill,
As a tale that is told.
But still returns Spring with her leaves
The flowers and light,
And walls that have seen so much,
Grow young overnight.

David Hope

SUNDAY—FEBRUARY 19.

I AND My Father are one.

MONDAY—FEBRUARY 20.

AN old man always had a habit of saying, "Yes! But it could have been worse." His friends, trying to cure him, got together and worked out an idea they thought would do the trick.

When they met again, one of them said, "Last night I dreamt I was in hell. It was so hot, so unbearable, it just couldn't have been worse!"

After listening, the old man scratched his brow and said, "Yes, but it could have been worse."

"How?" exclaimed the exasperated friend.

"Well, it could have been true!" the old man said quietly.

TUESDAY—FEBRUARY 21.

STANDING in front of me in the queue for the bus the other morning was a young schoolboy.

He was bursting over with happiness, singing and whistling cheerily. I overheard him remark to a friend that he and his pal were going to start work on a model aeroplane that evening.

He couldn't wait for school to be over.

And he set me wondering. Could such a little thing as that make and keep me happy all day?

There you have it. The question is whether it takes a little or a lot to make you happy.

It's a question worth thinking about. For on the answer depends whether you can really enjoy life.

You see, happiness need not be expensive, if only you know where to look for it.

It's there all around you in the form of the little things you see and do each and every day.

WEDNESDAY—FEBRUARY 22.

THOUGH winds are high and piercing cold,
I feel the summer sun,
And see the glowing isles of Greece
Ere history was begun . . .
Forgotten ways of ancient days,
On these with awe I look
As by the winter fire I sit, and
Read a travel book!

THURSDAY—FEBRUARY 23.

THE REV. PHILLIPS has for long been interested in the work being done for refugees.

From time to time he gives a talk to help bring home to his congregation the terrible plight of the thousands of people, young and old, who each year flee to freedom with only the clothes they wear.

While speaking about the Chinese refugees who have flooded on to the little island of Hong Kong, he held up a small jar for all to see. It contained a refugee's daily ration of rice. " How would you like to live for a day on this?" he asked.

After the service, Mr Phillips went home, not knowing what impression, if any, his talk had made.

Then a few days later a young couple—both in his parish, but not regular churchgoers—came to his house.

The young man said, " We heard your little sermon on the Chinese refugees in Hong Kong. We'd like you to send this money there." And he handed over 30s.

Maybe not a big sum, but what touched Mr Phillips most was that these two young people were newly married and struggling to furnish their new home, yet they were gladly making a sacrifice for total strangers thousands of miles away.

FRIDAY—FEBRUARY 24.

A BIG car pulled up at our door. A big man got out. He gave our bell a big ring; and when I came face to face with him he said:

"Remember me? I'm the man you came to see at midnight in hospital 10 years ago. The doctor and matron said I was dying, and my wife asked you to pay a visit. I've just looked you up to say I'm still going strong, and to apologise for getting you out of bed for nothing!"

Then he gave my hand a big squeeze and smiled a big smile.

Life's a queer business. All of us get dull and monotonous days . . . but now and then life is surprising, isn't it?

SATURDAY—FEBRUARY 25.

A LITTLE of the sunshine faded with the passing of Mrs Isa Lamond.

What a cheery, neighbourly soul she was! For years, though she lived alone and was far from well, she had a smile for everybody, fed the birds which came to her window, and kept her small kettle always on the boil to make a cup of tea for visitors.

And she helped *me* enormously, too.

She used to write the liveliest of letters, and always she popped in a few tea bags or a verse of her own composition or a dozen stamps!

"Here's a few more stamps, Francis," she would write. "Don't bother to reply—just send a comforting letter to some old body worse off than I am."

Those stamps *did* help, too. I used them as Isa Lamond wished. I felt I had to, for of her little she gave much; and if she could forget her own troubles and think of and bless others, why surely I could emulate her splendid example.

SUNDAY—FEBRUARY 26.

AND I say also unto thee, That thou art Peter, and upon this rock I will build My church; and the gates of hell shall not prevail against it.

MONDAY—FEBRUARY 27.

TO those with a heavy heart, this old verse may bring a little comfort and some renewal of faith.

Not till the loom is silent
And the shuttles cease to fly,
Will God unroll the canvas,
And explain the reason why
The dark threads are as useful
In the weaver's skilful hand
As the threads of gold and silver
In the pattern he has planned.

TUESDAY—FEBRUARY 28.

CAPTAIN JOHN has finished his course. He was seventy when he died—and died very calmly and, I think, very happily, at sunset one evening.

What an exciting life he'd had—travelling half-way round the world, winning two medals in the First World War, mentioned in despatches, doing risky things in the Middle East—he was a spy for a time, and later continually fighting verbal battles with local authorities.

And when the end was fast approaching he lay very still, looking at his wife. Was he fighting his battles again? Or travelling the road to Mandalay once more?

Not he. Almost his last words were: "Do you remember when we took that hot pie to Mr and Mrs Forbes, Mary?"

Surprising—or not?

MARCH

WEDNESDAY—MARCH 1.

MAY be you'll never be a hit,
Or be a big, big guy
Who's always making headlines hum
And in the public eye.

But if you are a friendly soul,
It's likely folk will say
That doing good just where you can
Is much the better way.

THURSDAY—MARCH 2.

EVER heard a sermon three miles long?

I did. I had attended the evening service and afterwards the minister and I decided to walk the long way home.

On the way, the minister said—" You know, I've always been meaning to preach on the Golden Rule—'All things whatsoever ye would that men should do to you, do ye even so to them.' But I doubt now if I ever shall. It's the plainest bit of good advice anybody ever gave anybody.

" Suppose, Francis, that everybody obeyed the Golden Rule—all of us treating all the rest as we'd like others to treat us. Gone would be all wars and the need for spending money on nuclear weapons; and half the pain and suffering would go, and we should all be infinitely happier and safer . . ."

So my friend went on for three miles, unconsciously preaching a sermon, and pondering on that curious twist in all our natures which somehow prevents us being what we want others to be, a twist which nothing can straighten except complete surrender to Christ.

FRIDAY—MARCH 3.

I PASS this on to you as it was passed on to me:

I asked for strength that I might achieve.
I was made weak that I might learn humbly to obey.
I asked for health that I might do greater things.
I was given infirmity that I might do better things.
I asked for riches that I might be happy.
I was given poverty that I might be wise.
I asked for power that I might have the praise of men.
I was given weakness that I might feel the need of God.
I asked for all things that I might enjoy life.
I was given life that I might enjoy all things.

SATURDAY—MARCH 4.

THE year is rolling on. There may be snow or fog tomorrow or there may be gales howling over the chimneys, but even so we are fast approaching the end of winter and coming nearer to springtime . . . singing birds and colour in the gardens and wonder and allurement out of doors and more daylight to thank God for.

A challenge to you who are gardeners—you'll be turning the good earth pretty soon and dreaming of your runner beans and your new potatoes.

This third month brings whispers to the ears of the Lady of the House . . . she's seen cobwebs already, and her fingers are itching to be at them. I believe she's positively longing to snatch up pail and brush and lead an attack upon dust and grime—a kind of mission in which she hopes to make her corner of the world a bit brighter.

March brings springtime and old folk have new hopes and young folk feel romantic as the weary world rushes out of darkness into sunshine.

SUNDAY—MARCH 5.

THE wind bloweth where it listeth, and thou hearest the sound thereof, but canst not tell whence it cometh, and whither it goeth: so is every one that is born of the Spirit.

MONDAY—MARCH 6.

"BY the way," said I to my schoolboy friend, "what does a glazier do when he hasn't any glass?"

That stumped the boy who lives across the road. He puzzled over my query till we reached the bus-stop. "Tell me." he begged.

"Drinks out of a cup," I replied.

I felt wickedly happy all the way home.

TUESDAY—MARCH 7.

WHEN you handed Kate Kelling your coppers you got much more than a newspaper . . . .

Every weekday for over forty years Kate set up her stall of orange boxes outside London's Bayswater Underground Station. It had been her newspaper pitch since she was a girl of 17; and between three in the afternoon and eight at night, rain, hail or shine, she handed out newspapers—and a smile of happiness—to everyone who stopped there.

One Monday Kate and her stall were missing from their usual spot . . . she had taken ill and died suddenly.

Then a lovely thing happened. First one, then another and another of her customers and friends, rich and poor, laid flowers on the pavement where she had served so long, until the pavement was ablaze with over 60 wreaths in tribute to her.

Kate was "only" a paper girl, but no one will know the sunshine she brought to so many.

WEDNESDAY—MARCH 8.

DEAR God, I kneel before Thee now,
A sinner and a sham,
Ashamed of many things I've done,
Ashamed of what I am.
But there is pardon for all guilt,
And love belongs to Thee.
Lord, by Thy grace make me more like
The man I meant to be!

THURSDAY—MARCH 9.

HOW often we say, "Oh, but it couldn't happen to me," without really thinking that it COULD happen—and does.

I had a letter from a woman who had said those very words—and yet not long ago she found herself visiting Craiginches Prison to see her son—at heart a good lad—who had gone off the rails in a moment of folly.

"*If only* he'd listened to me . . . *If only* he'd thought . . . *if only* he'd been more careful of his company. He was my son—yet this was like talking to a stranger. This was the lad who'd never done a dishonest thing in his life . . . the lad who'd been brought up to tell the truth and shame the devil . . .

"There he was, in prison clothes, trying to look happy.

"It was soon over. Fifteen minutes of trying to make sense out of small talk, and trying to keep hurt and anger out of it all. Silently he was taken away, the look in his eyes saying, 'You'll come back?'

"As I walked back to the gate I whispered to myself—'There's so much good in the worst of us, and so much bad in the best of us.'

"So all you young folk, remember the words 'if only,' before it's too late . . ."

BREAKFAST

One moment they're not there at all
But watch a moment now,
From all around they gather,
They must know somehow,
Worms are on the menu
When the ploughman starts to plough.

DAVID HOPE

THE CALL

We found you on the mountain bare,
Wrapped you round with loving care ;
In our home you are the king,
But Daddy says one day will bring
A scent from off the hills to say
" Come, come, away "—
And off you'll go.

DAVID HOPE

FRIDAY—MARCH 10.

DO let me share with you the story related in a recent issue of the Post Office Magazine.

It seems that a Scottish head postmaster, addressing his Rotary Club, told the story of a lady who complained while standing at a post office counter that the charge for sending a parcel was too much. "I never thought it would be such a lot," she declared.

"I'm sorry," murmured the polite counter clerk. He paused a moment, and then added brightly. "Of course, it could go at a cheaper rate if it were open at both ends."

"Why, you great daftie," snapped the customer, "it *is* open at both ends! It's my husband's trousers!"

SATURDAY—MARCH 11.

YOU'LL go far to find a happier man than Robert Hewitt. He's a small, wiry man, with face and arms the colour of polished mahogany.

Every morning, rain or shine, for 10 years he has been out on the road with his brush and shovel and handcart.

Everybody in the district knows Robbie and Robbie knows everybody—and many have good reason to bless him . . . a penny to a bairn on his way to school, a shilling to a man down on his luck.

Robbie hasn't a big wage as wages go, but he's forever dipping into his pocket to help those who travel along HIS road.

If you ask him why he's so happy, I doubt if he could tell you. But surely part of the secret is in his own simple philosophy—"If you can't help someone who's down on his luck, you're not much use to the world."

Many folk will envy Wee Robbie—in his humble way he has found contentment that they never find.

SUNDAY—MARCH 12.

AND in the fourth watch of the night Jesus went unto them, walking on the sea.

MONDAY—MARCH 13.

ONE Sunday morning a boy was given a sixpence and a threepenny-bit by his father.

"Put which you like in the collection-plate at church," the father told his son.

The boy went off to church and on his return home his father asked—"Well, which did you put in the collection—the sixpence or the threepenny-bit?"

His son was very frank in his reply. "At first," said he, "I thought I ought to give the sixpence, Dad. But luckily I remembered just in time that it says in the Bible—'The Lord loveth a cheerful giver.' I jolly well knew I'd enjoy giving the threepence, so that's what I did."

Boys will be boys!

TUESDAY—MARCH 14.

SUCH a lot of things to worry us in these days, aren't there? Riots here and there, strikes and accidents and stories of rebellious youth . . . and so on and so on.

And yet . . .

The musical rattle of tea cups; children laughing and playing; sunrise and sunset; the sea on a windy day or beneath a full moon; a book you don't want to put down; something on TV that grips you; a memory that warms the heart; the thrill of meeting a friend at a street corner; a hymn or song you simply cannot forget; a neighbour's kindness; a word of cheer; a little happy surprise . . . it's not such a bad world after all!

WEDNESDAY—MARCH 15.

WHEN your heart is breaking,
When you're crushed by care,
Cruel each awakening—
Waking to despair;
Hold on, hold on bravely,
And at any cost . . .
Hope when hope seems foolish,
All may NOT be lost!

THURSDAY—MARCH 16.

IT'S not always easy to be neighbourly when you've moved to a new district and don't know any of the people around you. The others are probably just as willing to be neighbourly as you are, but who's going to break the ice?

"Who better than the church?" thinks the Rev. W. Neilson Peterkin.

So members of his Bible class have delivered a neighbourly card to every home in his parish. One side of the card reads—"You need a break in the middle of the week." The other side has a message from the minister, who says—

"Dear Neighbour—Each Wednesday there will be a short service in Broom Church at 10.30 a.m. We shall be glad to see you if you are free. If you have young children, there will be a creche with playpens, toys and a qualified staff of assistants and a pram park.

"The service will last for 20 minutes and then you can get on with the shopping or the morning's engagements. But if you are free, we invite you for a cup of coffee in the hall. Come when you like, go when you like. I'm sure you'll be the better of a break on Wednesday."

Isn't that the neighbourly spirit?

FRIDAY—MARCH 17.

I WENT out without saying a word to my wife. I posted my letter at the pillar-box. Then I went further along the road towards the shops—and met her!

She looked lovely. I told her so, and she gave me a bewitching smile. I said I would walk along with her, and she said there was no objection to my doing so—if I would be pleased to carry her basket, which I did. She inquired why I was not at home, and I said I had been to post a letter; and she said, "Curious."

I said, "Not at all."

Then we looked at each other, and I was glad it was my own wife I'd fallen in love with and not somebody else's.

SATURDAY—MARCH 18.

DURING the last war, a church in Strasbourg was destroyed. Nothing remained except a heap of rubble and broken glass, or so the people thought till they began clearing away the masonry.

Then they found a statue of Christ still standing erect. In spite of all the bombing, it was unharmed except that both hands were missing.

Eventually rebuilding of the church began. One day a sculptor saw the figure of Christ, and offered to carve new hands. The church officials met to consider the sculptor's friendly gesture . . . and decided *not* to accept the offer.

Why? Because the members of that church said—"Our broken statue will serve to remind us that Christ touches the spirits of men, but that He has no hands to minister to the needy or feed the hungry or enrich the poor—except *our* hands. He inspires. We perform."

SUNDAY—MARCH 19.

FOR I have given you an example that ye should do as I have done to you.

MONDAY—MARCH 20.

CAME home the other evening and found a hot tea all ready, and the Lady of the House full of news and views—she always is after having been shopping for half an hour. She had changed a library book, it seems; and while choosing another she had been glancing through a book by Mary Buckley. In it she found a sentence she had copied into her notebook . . . and she read it to me at tea:

"Husbands are awkward things to deal with—even keeping them in hot water doesn't make them tender!"

"H'm," said I.

TUESDAY—MARCH 21.

THERE are some people in this world who are only too ready with an excuse.

I am sure you have met some of them. They are the type who could have been at the top, but, so they'll tell you, they did not have the time nor the facilities for study.

But the fact is that nobody gets anywhere or achieves anything worthwhile without some measure of effort, sacrifice and determination.

The real excuse for those who fail is that they did not have the courage and persistence needed to make a success.

Whatever task is ahead of you, you've got to keep on till it's done.

If you don't, you may one day find yourself one of the self-pitying set who have to make excuses.

WEDNESDAY—MARCH 22.

AN itch in the fingers,
An eye on the dust,
An influx of painters—
To hubby's disgust;
A rush of springitis,
Hot water galore . . .
Let's clean every bedroom
And sleep on the floor!

THURSDAY—MARCH 23.

ALTHOUGH it's some time since George Bisset passed on in his 82nd year, I've been thinking a good deal about him.

Life was very unkind to him. All his sons were at the war, and he and his wife worried about them—his wife so much that she suffered from blood pressure and eventually lost her memory.

Nothing was ever easy for George, and in later years he was nearly crippled with rheumatism. For the last four years he visited his wife in hospital as regularly as clockwork, though nobody will ever know what it cost him in physical exertion.

And when he reached the bedside it was heart-breaking to see the tears running down his cheeks, for his wife did not even know him. Yet a faint smile from her was reward enough.

George might so easily have railed against God, and cursed the ills of his life, but he never did. Instead, he kept on bravely and hopefully every day, worshipped by children, admired by friends . . .

Not all the philosophers of past and present can explain why life is easy for some and hard for others . . . but making the best of things with a smile and a touch of graciousness is surely the best argument against the slings and arrows of outrageous fortune.

Friday—March 24.

I HAPPENED to hear this story of Sir Norman Birkett the other day. Few, if any British judges of recent years have had a more brilliant career, and perhaps there has never been one with a more agile mind.

On one occasion Sir Norman was guest of honour at a gathering of surgeons, and in his after-dinner speech he remarked with his usual dry humour that he had no idea why he had been invited to such an occasion, since the law and surgery were obviously poles apart. "After I have finished with a case," went on Sir Norman, "I wonder what I have left out. When *you* have finished with a case you wonder if you have left anything in."

Saturday—March 25.

I'M sure the congregation of Hill Kirk had never seen the like before.

It happened at the christening of little John Alexander Shanks. The congregation were singing the baptismal hymn, expecting any minute to see a godmother bringing the baby to the font.

But suddenly a door opened and a *man* came in, carrying the baby!

He was Mr John Lewis, and he marched right down the aisle towards the font and waited for the minister to begin the christening.

Four years ago, when the baby's mother, Mrs Joan Shanks, was married, it was her uncle, Mr Lewis, who gave her away. She felt he was her godfather.

So when the baby was born he was named after Mr Lewis, and it was arranged that Mr Lewis should carry the baby to the christening.

A happy thought from a happy family.

SUNDAY—MARCH 26.

ON the next day much people that were come to the feast, when they heard that Jesus was coming to Jerusalem, took branches of palm trees, and went forth to meet Him, and cried, Hosanna: Blessed is the King of Israel that cometh in the name of the Lord.

MONDAY—MARCH 27.

I'D like you to picture for a moment the darkened room of a quiet London house.

A man lies seriously ill, and for days and nights on end his brother has hardly left the bedside.

The man who sat by the bed was Sir Arthur Sullivan, the famous composer.

For years already, the comic operas of Gilbert and Sullivan had charmed the world—but now Sullivan's face was lined with sorrow and his eyes were heavy with tears. He knew his brother Frederick had not long to live.

At last Sir Arthur tried to snatch a few minutes' rest, but rest was impossible. He was weary and ill at ease . . . and the words of a song came back to him—words he'd tried for four years to set to music, and failed: " Seated one day at the organ, I was weary and ill at ease . . ."

Now, in his distress, a new melody ran through his mind—a tune of simple beauty—and there and then, as his brother lay dying, Sir Arthur wrote the noble music of " The Lost Chord."

" It flooded the crimson twilight,
Like the close of an angel's psalm.
And it lay on my fevered spirit
With a touch of infinite calm . . ."

Even if he had written nothing more, Sir Arthur Sullivan's name would be remembered always.

TUESDAY—MARCH 28.

IT'S one of those moments Mrs Robinson will never forget!

Her daughter, Joyce, and George Mason, had their wedding all planned when, alas, Mrs Robinson had to go into hospital.

A bigger disappointment would be hard to think of, yet Mrs Robinson, mother-like, wouldn't hear of the wedding being postponed because of her.

So the big day dawned. The young couple were married and off they went to greet their guests at the reception.

But they weren't finished yet. According to plan, they were whisked off to the City Hospital.

A nurse struck up the "Wedding March" on a piano specially wheeled in for the occasion—and in swept the newly-weds, arm-in-arm, just as they'd walked from the kirk!

I'm sure the tears of joy weren't far from Mrs Robinson's eyes as she sat up in bed, specially dressed for the occasion, and watched her daughter and her new son-in-law coming up the ward to her bedside.

Thank you, Joyce and George, and thank you, matron and nurses, for turning what could have been a day of disappointment into one whose memories Mrs Robinson will always treasure.

WEDNESDAY—MARCH 29.

WHEN the heart is near to breaking,
Rough your lonely road,
Hope extinguished, joy forgotten,
Grief and pain your load . . .
Plod on bravely through the darkness,
Groping all the way,
Till God brings you to the sunshine
Of a brighter day.

THURSDAY—MARCH 30.

I MUST tell you about Mary's bowl of flowers.

She started growing them in September. At that time they were just lifeless-looking narcissi bulbs.

Mary tended them carefully until, in time, there was the most perfect bowl of narcissi you ever saw.

Yet Mary herself has never seen them . . . she is blind. This didn't stop her—and others like her—sending their flowers to a show.

It was a moving experience to see Mary and her friends passing round the tables and bending forward to touch and appraise the blooms before them. And they smiled as the fragrance rose, fresh and sweet.

Oh, yes—I almost forgot to tell you. There is something new on the sideboard along with Mary's bowl of flowers, a silver cup. Well done, Mary!

FRIDAY—MARCH 31.

IT'S almost Easter Sunday.

Has it any message for you?

Easter Sunday follows Good Friday. The anniversary of gloom and suffering and defeat (as it seemed) is followed by the triumphant day of rejoicing and victory.

There is, I think, another message:—

It is that we can begin again.

Christ died and rose again. So may we die in the sense that we are finished with our old way of living, and so may we be resurrected in the sense that we can begin living a new and a better life.

If then, as the church bells ring, you feel that you will finish with the old, unsatisfactory way of life and will begin living more finely—make that great decision now, so that on this Easter Sunday what is unworthy in you may die and what is good and lovely may be born afresh.

APRIL

Saturday—April 1.

IT would warm your heart to hear Mrs Cotton talk about her 26 boys.

For they'll always be boys to her, just as they seemed that day years ago when she first met them . . .

It was in Linburn House, which had just been opened for Scottish war blinded, and the first 26 men had arrived to learn to build new lives in their darkness. How young they seemed, so like her own boy, who only the year before had been killed with the R.A.F., aged 20.

Mrs Cotton was told to stand at one end of a big room. In her hand she had 26 books of savings certificates, each worth £8 5s and bearing a man's name.

As each name was called, a man walked forward towards the sound, still hesitant in his new world of blindness. It was all Mrs Cotton could do not to go forward and stretch out a hand . . . she knew then why she had been told to stand still, but it was a hard task for a mother.

Oh, yes, each man got £8 5s as his personal gift, and that was only a beginning. By the time the last of the 26 had passed through Linburn, Mrs Cotton and her band of faithful helpers had bought them nearly 2000 savings certificates.

I know, also, she has already had her reward in helping these 26 boys.

You see, she did it as a memorial to her own son.

Sunday—April 2.

AND, behold, there was a great earthquake : for the angel of the Lord descended from heaven, and came and rolled back the stone from the door and sat upon it.

MONDAY—APRIL 3.

THIS is the story of Joe's sepulchre.

Every Easter he builds it in the lovely grounds of St Thomas's Church, in the heart of Newcastle. He spends hours and days carefully fashioning the low-arched entrance, setting stone upon stone for the walls, and building up earth and turf on which flowers grow. On top, he places the three wooden crosses of Calvary, and finally, he closes the entrance with a great stone.

Then, lo, when Newcastle awakes on Easter Day, the stone has been rolled aside, and within the empty sepulchre there lies the final testimony—a scrap of white cloth, discarded, mute, yet telling all . . .

I don't think I've heard a more beautiful way of telling the story of Easter.

TUESDAY—APRIL 4.

IT'S all my eye and little apples, friends.

Yes, and you can say it from me to the next person who starts to tell you that young folk nowadays think only of themselves.

Take a young couple I know in Grangemouth, for instance. Not so long ago they became engaged, and oh, how happy they were.

Now, you would think if any young people had cause to forget everybody but their own two selves, it was these newly-engaged sweethearts.

Yet, what did they do? Instead of going out to celebrate, they sent the money they would have spent to the Glasgow and District Coast Homes at Saltcoats—to provide someone with a week's holiday!

You see, these two young people felt their happiness so overflowing they simply HAD to share it.

Bless their hearts for the lovely—and quite original—way they did it.

WEDNESDAY—APRIL 5.

IT isn't really what goes wrong,
What ills you have to bear,
How hard each day, how rough the way,
How great your load of care.
The thing that matters most of all
Is do you whine or grin;
Are you a gallant, cheery soul
Refusing to give in?
A bit of pluck, a smile, a song
Will bring you through when things go wrong!

THURSDAY—APRIL 6.

MRS LANG was walking home from church one Sunday last year when a car drew up alongside her. It was her neighbours, the Cumming family.

Mrs Cumming laughed as they set off again. " We almost weren't at church today," she said. " Paul heard the bells just as we were going to sit down to breakfast—and we had to leave it and run. We forgot to put the clock forward !"

Mrs Lang smiled, without really taking her neighbour literally.

But when they all arrived at the Cummings' home, David, aged five, begged Mrs Lang to come in to see his pet hamsters—so in she went. And there in the kitchen, to her surprise, she saw a neatly-laid table, and on the stove five shining white plates, each containing a congealed fried egg and bacon !

Not a fork or knife had been so much as lifted, for as soon as the family had heard the bells, and realised they were an hour behind, they'd dropped everything and hurried to get ready for the kirk !

As I looked at *my* bacon and eggs I doubted if *I'd* have had the heart to leave them—as the Cummings did !

FRIDAY—APRIL 7.

A BOY went to a party at which a conjurer did some tricks which mystified his audience beyond all telling. "Gosh," exclaimed a little girl after the conjurer had lifted a lovely white rabbit out of an empty hat, "that's wizard."

"Oh, I don't know," remarked the wee lad. "My dad can bring tulips out of a bowl of soil!"

It's the growing season, isn't it? If only you and I were not quite so used to it, should we not think of springtime as a sort of huge conjuring trick—a miraculous feat whereby gardeners change soil and water and fresh air and sunshine into tulips and wall-flowers and roses and so much loveliness of form and colour and fragrance that summer's over and gone before we have time to see or enjoy even half of it?

SATURDAY—APRIL 8.

SEVEN-year-old Daren was going home from school one wet and windy night. Just as she crossed the grass verge outside her house, the lid of her little case flew open, and out fell her school books and things. Hurriedly she picked them up and ran indoors.

But when she got in she discovered her pencil sharpener was missing. "And it was such a nice sharpener," Daren said tearfully.

Next morning she rose early and ran out to have another look for her treasure. Bless me, if she didn't come running in with it a few seconds later!

"I suddenly remembered I hadn't prayed about it," she said to her mother. "So I told God, and asked Him to look with me . . . and He did . . . and so I found it!"

It makes me wonder how many joys we older folk might find if we but had the faith and trust of a little child.

SUNDAY—APRIL 9.

BY much slothfulness the building decayeth; and through idleness of the hands the house droppeth through.

MONDAY—APRIL 10.

ROBERT LOUIS STEVENSON—feeling the call of spring—once wrote: "I am told there are people who do not care for maps . . . The names, shapes of woodlands, the courses of roads and rivers, the mills and the ruins, the ponds and the ferries, perhaps the Standing Stone or the Druids' Circle on the heath . . . here is an inexhaustible fund of interest for anyone with eyes to see or twopenny-worth of imagination."

TUESDAY—APRIL 11.

THIS is one of the happiest stories I have ever been able to tell. It concerns the Rev. Redvers Anderson, a minister who recently went through an operation that would either restore his failing sight—or take it away altogether.

One night after the operation, Mr Anderson awoke with a searing pain in his eye. Was this, he wondered, the blindness he had been dreading?

A wave of despair surged over him. Then he began to pray—". . . if it be thy will, O Lord, so let it be . . ."

Mr Anderson tells me that just as suddenly as the pain came, it left him, and in place of despair came a wonderful peace and calm. In that moment he was sure his sight was restored.

Now Mr Anderson sees clearly the things he has only seen dimly for years . . . the faces of his loved ones . . . the beauty of his garden in the evening sun . . . the glory of the countryside.

Wednesday—April 12.

SAD it is so many folk
Grief and sorrow know,
Troubled are with fears and doubts
Till the hot tears flow;
Broken hearts and shattered dreams—
Life can hurt so much, it seems.

Glad am I if folk distressed
Have a friend to share
Some or all the ills that come—
Ills so hard to bear.
Happy you if folk who're sad
Turn to YOU to make them glad!

Thursday—April 13.

THE nurse was in a hurry. She opened the door of the ante-room to the ward and walked in without knocking.

She stopped, puzzled. Then she tiptoed out. For in the corner of the room, on his knees, was her chief, a leading surgeon. Why was he praying?

That afternoon he had operated on a little boy, and during the operation the boy's heart had stopped beating. No one panicked. Surgeons and nurses never do. But with infinite patience and tenderness the surgeon started massaging the boy's heart . . . He had a son of his own just that age.

At last the tiny heart gave a gentle whisper. With renewed hope, the medical team strove on until one hour later the heart had picked up a regular, steady rhythm. The danger was over.

But the incident wasn't. Thanks had to be given to One whose presence is always very real to that surgeon at the operating table. That's why the nurse found him on his knees.

A SHEPHERD'S CROOK

The expert saw it growing,
With a hundred other sticks,
He cut it and he shaped it
By a dozen artful tricks.
And now it's fit to pass the test
Of men who know—and need—the best.

DAVID HOPE

WASHING-UP

There's many would be champions
And win a silver cup,
But there's never competition
When it comes to washing-up !

DAVID HOPE

Friday—April 14.

I FOUND this verse written on a £1 note. It bears thinking about.

"This piece of paper in your hand
Declares to you that on demand,
You twenty shillings shall receive.
This simple promise you believe.
It sets your heart as much at rest
As if the silver you possessed.
So Christ Who died, but now doth live,
Doth unto you this promise give—
That if you on His name believe,
You shall eternal life receive.
Upon the first you surely rest.
Which is the safest and the best?
The bank may break, Heaven never can.
'Tis safer trusting God than man."

Saturday—April 15.

I LOOKED at the socks . . . and I thought how every stitch was touched with wonder.

I pictured Maggie Baird's quiet little room where she knitted them.

Maggie often goes to bed early and knits in the dark. You see, she doesn't need the light, for she has only the slightest bit of sight at the corner of one eye. She's also stone deaf.

Yet what a wonderful soul she is. She's interested in everything—knitting, making rugs and flowers, cooking, cleaning and popping off eight miles to do her shopping. Her little figure is so smart and sprightly that folk have to look twice to realise she's carrying a white stick.

Yes, that's Maggie, who works away and sings to herself, yet neither hears nor sees. Yet she thanks God for His many blessings . . .

SUNDAY—APRIL 16.

AND as Moses lifted up the serpent in the wilderness, even so must the Son of Man be lifted up: That whosoever believeth in Him should not perish, but have eternal life.

MONDAY—APRIL 17.

ONLY very simple people think themselves clever because they can find something wrong.

Believe me, finding fault, seeing what's ugly, spotting other people's mistakes is easier than falling out of bed, and the most accomplished expert at the job has just nothing whatever to boast of.

On the other hand, it does take skill and faith and quickness of perception and a genius for cheerfulness to find the good.

It isn't easy, folks . . . but it's one of the most rewarding things any of us can ever do.

TUESDAY—APRIL 18.

STAN CHARLTON hurt his knee when pushing his car. How could Stan, or anyone, know that such a little thing would change his life?

Alas, it did. The leg became worse. Stan had to give up his career as a sea-going engineer. And, despite all that could be done, the infirmity spread.

Today, Stan is so completely paralysed he cannot wiggle a toe or move a finger. He lies day and night in a double bed. His TV opposite the foot of the bed, is on a special bracket near the ceiling so that he can just see . . .

" There are many cases worse off than me," Stan says. " After all, how many men of my age are still blessed with a wonderful mother?"

Surely the words of a gallant gentleman.

Wednesday—April 19.

DEAR Lord, excuse my heavy boots,
My dungarees and cap,
I'm praying on my way to work,
For I'm a working chap.
The bus is just ahead, but, Lord,
I've surely time to pray
For strength to be a better man
Than I was yesterday.

Thursday—April 20.

IF you want to know what joy a little thought can bring, ask Mary Ann.

When she answered her door she was puzzled to find a tall stranger in the uniform of the Salvation Army. He carried a bunch of flowers and a parcel.

"Mary Ann?" he asked kindly. She nodded. "You have a birthday today, haven't you?" he went on, and Mary Ann was so surprised it was out before she could stop. "My 71st!" she said proudly.

"Then I wish you many happy returns from the Salvation Army—and from your daughter and grandson in Australia," said the visitor with a smile.

With that he gallantly presented the flowers and helped her to unwrap the parcel. In it was a beautiful iced birthday cake with the greeting, "Happy Birthday, Granny."

You'll have guessed, of course, that Mary Ann's daughter was behind the birthday surprise. She didn't want Granny to put any gift she might send into the housekeeping money and not use it for herself. So she sent money to the Salvation Army and asked them to buy flowers and a birthday cake and deliver them on the right day.

She hoped it would bring joy—and I can assure her with all my heart that it did.

FRIDAY—APRIL 21.

"TIME and time again," she told me, "my husband and I talked of moving house. He's been doing well this last six years, and the only thing he and I have longed for was a house with a garden . . . but as long as his mother was alive we felt we *must* stay in this dull old place. You see, every day one of us wheeled her into the front room so that she could see the children going to school or coming away. She just loved to watch them and hear them shouting. And, of course, she waved to them. They helped her to keep young in spirit."

SATURDAY—APRIL 22.

I THINK Mrs Heath could truthfully have said she was sorry to be going home from hospital. While she'd been there, she had had every kindness and attention, and, above all, she had had company. For Mrs Heath is a widow, and lives alone.

That's why she wasn't looking forward to going back home, I think. For as she travelled back across the city in the ambulance, she told the nursing sister that there wouldn't be a soul to welcome her, and her house would be cold and cheerless.

But, wonder of wonders! When the ambulance drew up at her door, Mrs Heath heard a strong voice hailing her. "Come away in," said the voice. "There's a fire on inside, and the kettle's on for a cup of tea!"

Of course, Mrs Heath couldn't believe her ears—until she saw it was her minister who had called to her. Unbeknown to her, he had got the key of her house, found out when she was due back, and laid on a warm welcome-home surprise.

Somehow, for old Mrs Heath, that homecoming wasn't half as bad as she'd imagined it would be—thanks to an understanding friend.

SUNDAY—APRIL 23.

AS the Father hath loved Me, so have I loved you: continue ye in My love.

MONDAY—APRIL 24.

IF you and I are to see anything of the freshness and loveliness of this season, hear anything of the music out of doors, catch anything of the thrill and wonder and joy of this magic time—well, the sooner the better. Gardens and lanes, fields and woods and murmuring streams are all luring us out of doors at the moment. There are birds and trees and flowers to delight us. Maybe we are so very busy we simply cannot spare an evening for a walk in the country. Perhaps we are too ill to adventure from our room. But if by any chance we *can* walk into wonderland—let's do so before the freshness goes.

TUESDAY—APRIL 25.

IN 1915 a telegram came for young Mrs Devon. Her husband had been killed in France, leaving her with three children to bring up.

Not long afterwards another young mother, Mrs McNeill, heard that her husband, too, had fallen.

What hand drew these two sorrowing women together, I can only guess—for until then they were total strangers. But in each other they found comfort and strength to keep on.

Why, the courage they seemed to gain from each other took them into other bereaved homes, where they were able to bring some of the peace they themselves had found.

The splendid thing is that after all those years they still meet every Monday to share each other's troubles and joys.

WEDNESDAY—APRIL 26.

IF a trouble hits you hard
You can weep all day,
Moan and groan until you're ill—
Sigh your soul away.
Better far to battle on
Wear a gallant smile,
Keep on somehow—God knows HOW—
Mile on weary mile . . .
Till you come to joy at last,
All your worries long since past!

THURSDAY—APRIL 27.

DAN ARNISON had been without a steady job for thirteen years.

Then he brought his wife and little girl to Darlington to seek work. The only home they could find was dingy and damp. Dan's heart sank when he saw it, and his wife found it hard to hold back the tears.

It was just then, when things looked blackest, Dan remembered his mother's words—if he needed help to go on his knees and ask for it.

So there, among their few bits of furniture and belongings, Dan and his wife knelt on the stone floor and prayed.

They hardly got back to their feet when there was a knock on the door. A complete stranger stood there. She had heard them arrive and something prompted her to ask if all was well.

Remarkable as it seems, from that moment all was well, indeed, with Dan. Three days later he was picked from 46 people as the tenant of a nice house. Not only that, he soon found a job.

All through his life Dan has found his mother's words are true—if you ask for help in prayer, it will be given you.

FRIDAY—APRIL 28.

"WOW!" cried the excited schoolboy, staring at a passing car. "It's a Rolls! Gosh, betcher he's a millionaire! Wish I was!"

"See that boy on the pavement," remarked the owner of the Rolls to his chauffeur, "the slim laddie with the bright eyes? I fancy he doesn't know what indigestion is. I'd like to change places with him!"

SATURDAY—APRIL 29.

WHAT a great girl is Muriel Schofield.

I think she must be the only girl who uses a sweeping broom to help in cleaning her teeth, washing her face and even to dress.

You're amazed? So was I, until I found that Muriel's broom is a symbol of her courage, too.

You see, Muriel is crippled with arthritis. She can only walk across her room with the greatest effort. Worse still, she has lost almost all use of her hands.

With her feet steadying the broom-head on the floor, she uses the handle as a kind of dressing stand on which she hangs garments and wriggles into them. For washing, an elastic band on the handle holds a face cloth or tooth brush. She once even tried a cooking fork fixed to the handle—but that was too much!

A friend of mine met Muriel and it seems they spent most of the time laughing uproariously at the antics with the broom. For despite everything, Muriel refuses to be sorry for herself.

Yes, as I say, a great girl is Muriel.

SUNDAY—APRIL 30.

FOR what is a man profited, if he shall gain the whole world, and lose his own soul? Or what shall a man give in exchange for his soul?

MAY

MONDAY—MAY 1.

ARE you shocked?

I mean about the tale of the schoolboy who recently bought a bicycle with money he had been saving up for over three years.

Was he excited? He bought the bike one Saturday morning. On Friday night he went to bed—and knelt by his bed and said a wee prayer. " Bless Mum and Dad and Jean," said he reverently, " and make me a good boy. Oh, and by the way, God, if You want to see a smashing bike, You come with me in the morning!" That tale doesn't shock me.

The fact is, I've heard far too many prayers which were just people telling God their troubles. How refreshing for the Almighty to have a bit of good news from a lively schoolboy! Maybe there's a hint here for me!

TUESDAY—MAY 2.

THE Lady of the House and Mrs Scott happened to talk about a mutual acquaintance.

" Oh," exclaimed Mrs Scott, " there's some folk wouldn't be happy in heaven!"

When she came home, the Lady of the House shared this phrase with me. And how true it is.

Some folk are always complaining, aren't they? Take them to Switzerland and they'll be worrying because they don't remember pulling the living-room curtains before leaving home. Say a word in praise of somebody . . . and they'll be finding fault with him or her. They're discontented, envious, restless, awkward . . .

Depend on it, they wouldn't be happy in heaven!

You're sure you're not like that, aren't you?

FAITH

Our journey on life's highway,
Faith only can direct,
And show us how to overcome
The snags we don't expect.

D

DAVID HOPE

MEMORY

For healing there's the mountain air,
For music waters flowing
For rest the springy heather bed
For scent bog myrtle blowing ;

For candlelight Orion shines,
Reflected in the river—
I see it plain as long ago
For rich is memory's quiver.

David Hope

PLANTING POTATOES

Oh, it's bend, bend, bend,
Till you're fit to break your back!
Then comes the welcome signal,
And we tuck into our snack.
We stretch to take our ease
Have a friendly gossip, then,
Before we know what's happened,
Why, it's time to start again!

DAVID HOPE

WEDNESDAY—MAY 3.

AS I was going to work at dawn
I fell in step with Jim.
He seemed downhearted, so I said
A cheery word to him.
I didn't talk an awful lot—
But merely shared the grief he'd got.

As I was coming home one night,
A night both cold and drear,
Jim fell in step with me, and said
A welcome word of cheer.
And how my heart was warmed that he
Should share the fear which worried me!

THURSDAY—MAY 4.

ONE day in 1802 a young student sat in an examination room at Cambridge University.

Round about him were other students—all hard at work, afraid they wouldn't have time to finish before the bell rang.

But the pale, thin student was sitting back in his chair, wondering how to fill in the remaining half-hour—he had finished his mathematics but couldn't leave till all were dismissed.

So this young man—who died when only 21—used those precious moments to write on the back of his question paper!

He was Henry Kirke White, and what he wrote on that occasion was the now-famous hymn :—

Oft in danger, oft in woe,
Onward, Christians, onward go.
Fight the fight, maintain the strife,
Strengthened with the Bread of Life.

Every spare minute of your life is a challenge—use it as best you can !

FRIDAY—MAY 5.

IT was a dreadful experience . . .

David, eight years old, as fit as could be one day—and the next day so very ill.

They rushed him to hospital, and for days and days his life hung in the balance.

Meanwhile, Mum at home was just about distracted. David was all in all to her, her only child—and she could do nothing for him except wait and wait.

Every minute seemed a lifetime of agony . . . yet the odd thing is—Mum never once cried.

Often she came near to tears, but she kept on doing what had to be done, until that wonderful day when, so casually, a nurse said—" I think David will be coming home tomorrow."

Then Mum cried. She sobbed as if her heart would break. Ridiculous, wasn't it? But you'll understand.

SATURDAY—MAY 6.

I'M not surprised Mrs Radcliff believes in miracles.

For some time she has been practically an invalid and had to be carried downstairs to her wheel-chair and upstairs to her bed at night.

One night in bed she woke up and smelled smoke. She called out to her son. He dashed downstairs. To his horror he found the kitchen in flames.

At once the young man tackled the blaze, but soon he became aware someone was beside him, helping. It was his mother!

It was only then Mrs Radcliff realised what she had actually done. Without help, she had got out of bed where she had lain so helpless, walked downstairs, gone to her son's aid—and she couldn't even remember how she did it.

Yes, Mrs Radcliff believes in miracles. And after all, she should know . . .

SUNDAY—MAY 7.

AND he that taketh not his cross, and followeth after Me, is not worthy of Me.

MONDAY—MAY 8.

ARE you losing heart? Are you beginning to feel that it's no use trying any longer? Are you wondering if there's a hoodoo on you?

My friend, consider this: Suppose you lose your nerve and all your courage goes and you give up the battle against heavy odds, what then? Nothing but disaster.

Which means to say that, whether you like it or not, you've just *got* to keep on and on and on . . . and as long as you keep on there's a chance that things may improve in unexpected ways, that your luck will turn, that life will compensate you for your suffering.

And you need never keep on and on *alone*, for God always comes to the aid of those who turn to Him.

TUESDAY—MAY 9.

IT all started when the old lady heard Mr Gordon talking about the plight of refugees. She went home, thought about it, and realised that there were others far worse off than she was.

So she called the minister to her home, told him she wanted to give some money to the refugees, and asked him to suggest a suitable sum.

Knowing she wasn't too well off, Mr Gordon tentatively suggested a pound. But she shook her head. " More than that," she said. So the minister doubled the figure. Again she shook her head. Thus the bids mounted pound by pound, until at £20 the old lady nodded. " I'll give you £20," she murmured.

And, bless her, she did !

WEDNESDAY—MAY 10.

EVERYTHING going wrong today?
Everybody mad?
Life depressing as can be?
That is very sad.
What's the use of keeping on
When the fun and thrill are gone?

Just a minute though—perhaps
If tomorrow you
Get up looking for the best,
Trying hard to do
All the good you can . . . and smile,
Life may prove to be worthwhile!

THURSDAY—MAY 11.

WHAT a wonderful bit of overtime Tommy Rackley, the blacksmith, is putting in.

Ever since he left school Tommy has worked in Sunderland, making cranes that go all over the world.

Why mention him here? Because for two years Tommy and two of his mates spent part of every dinner break reading and discussing the Bible in a little hut on the works' ash dump.

Indeed, Tommy found it did him such a power of good that, with the co-operation of the management, he arranged proper meetings.

So now once a week, Tommy leads a meeting in what he calls his Church in the Works.

They meet for half an hour in a room, surrounded by diagrams, models and bits of machinery. And in that short time they are able to withdraw from the noise and bustle of the works for a Bible reading, a prayer and quiet meditation.

As I say, what a splendid bit of overtime he is putting in!

FRIDAY—MAY 12.

YOU hear things if you don't talk.

The Lady of the House and I spent a night in an East Coast hotel, and we happened to be sitting in the lounge thinking about going up to bed when we couldn't help overhearing two old dears having a heart-to-heart talk in voices which seemed to us unnecessarily loud.

"You know," said one, "it really upset me. I mean, I've been in and out of his shop thousands of times. I've known him for years—and then he goes off with another woman like that!"

"Well, of all things!" exclaimed the other old dear. "It must have been a shock . . ."

We had to smile of course . . . but on the way upstairs the Lady of the House said—"I wonder if I really know you, Francis?"

I wonder if she does? I wonder if I do? We are all such strange jumbles of complexes, aren't we?

That old dear thought she had known the wicked shopkeeper for years . . . but had she?

SATURDAY—MAY 13.

THIS cheery little bit of philosophy comes my way from an old lady in America :—

Since I have retired from life's competition,
I busy myself with complete repetition.
I get up each morning, dust off my wits,
Pick up the paper and read the obits,
If my name is missing, I know I'm not dead—
So I eat a good breakfast and go back to bed.

SUNDAY—MAY 14.

HE keepeth the paths of judgment, and preserveth the way of His saints.

MONDAY—MAY 15.

HAVE you heard this simple story of Clara Barton, founder of the American Red Cross?

Clara had come under much criticism for her beliefs, but had borne it all bravely.

Then one day a friend reminded her of a particularly mean trick that had been played on her. Clara looked puzzled, and her friend was amazed.

"Surely you remember that, Clara!" she cried.

Clara turned to her and said quietly but firmly—

"No, I distinctly remember forgetting that!"

TUESDAY—MAY 16.

FRIEND, when you come to the end of your pilgrimage—as come you must, one day—and you watch the sun going down for the last time, you will think precious little of money or houses or land, and any honours or titles you may have picked up along the journey will seem singularly cheap.

Most likely, in those clear last hours, what will comfort you most will be memories of the little kindnesses you've done and had done to you; the gentle words spoken; the burdens shouldered for others, the friendly bits of conversation by the way.

Consider this.

WEDNESDAY—MAY 17.

PITY the folk who just cannot let up:
Men more or less rushed off their feet,
Women who always find something to do,
And scarcely have patience to eat.
Here's to the people with courage enough
Sometimes to relax and be still,
To potter awhile—do nothing and smile,
And then set to work with a will!

THURSDAY—MAY 18.

"I'D like to add that I have a very great deal to be thankful for. I am rich. I am content. I have lots of friends. Could anybody want more?"

Now you might think such words came at the end of a letter from a millionaire or a lady who glitters with diamonds every evening.

My correspondent is, in fact, in an eventide home.

She is well on the way to being 80. Her possessions are few. Her income isn't worth mentioning. Yet a lot of people, far better off, might envy her!

It's exciting meeting anybody who is really happy—and a bit disturbing, too. You begin to ask yourself awkward questions. For instance—This happy old soul hasn't half the things I have, and cannot lead a life a quarter as exciting as mine is. What's her secret—and why isn't it mine?

I'm not going to try to answer those questions . . . I'm just leaving you to think about her and to make quite sure you are seeking after the truly worthwhile things of this life.

FRIDAY—MAY 19.

AFTER 50 years' banking experience, Mr John Anderson still delights in this story of a man and his money.

One day in the bank Mr Anderson briskly counted out a bundle of notes for an old farmer.

But the old chap at once began to count them again, carefully peeling off each note and laying it on the counter. Only when he was finished did he notice Mr Anderson still watching him. He was unabashed.

"Aye count y'r money," he said firmly, "even aifter y'r ain faither. No' that he'd cheat. He might mak' a mistake!"

SATURDAY—MAY 20.

THE minister asked the children for another word for happiness. The word he wanted was JOY.

Then he told the children to take each letter from JOY—J for Jesus, O for Others and Y for Yourself.

The secret of happiness is, of course, found in putting Jesus first, others next and yourself last.

Neat, isn't it?

SUNDAY—MAY 21.

LYING lips are an abomination to the Lord: but they that deal truly are His delight.

MONDAY—MAY 22.

I HAVE just heard of a band of Aberdeen housewives who count their blessings every six months—and then pass them on to others !

The women—20 of them—are members of South Church, and in each of their homes stands a little tin box. They're called " Thank you " boxes.

Well, here's what happens.

After the bairns are away to school in the morning and the menfolk are off to work, the mothers at last have time to think. And when they do think, why, as often as not their thoughts go something like this—" I've a lot to be thankful for—we've a grand family, a nice wee house, and there's the new rug in the sitting-room now." Or, " Thank goodness, John's got over his 'flu now."

So they pop a copper or two into the " Thank you " box just because everything is going so well.

Every six months all the boxes are opened together.

They are counted and then passed over to the church, to bring blessings to those who have few or no blessings to count.

TRY YOUR LUCK!

Walk up, walk up and have a go!
How good you are you'll never know,
In life or at a fairground shy
Till you've made up your mind to try.

DAVID HOPE

NOW DAY IS DONE

Now gone the sun
And day has run
Its course for joy or sorrow,
Let us ask at His hand
Forgiveness and
A chance to do better tomorrow.

DAVID HOPE

TUESDAY—MAY 23.

A FRIEND was visiting an old man in hospital. The patient had been in a good deal of pain and his visitor asked if they gave him sleeping pills to help him.

"No," replied the old man. "They don't give me sleeping pills—but I've brought my own!"

Then he turned and drew something from beneath his pillow. It was—a plain black Bible, and he held it up before the visitor's eyes. "My sleeping pills are in here," he smiled. "Isaiah, chapter 26, verse 3, and Psalm 4, verse 8. They've never failed me yet."

His visitor was now very curious. So she took the Book and turned up the verses. Here is what she read in Isaiah, "Thou wilt keep him in perfect peace, whose mind is stayed on Thee, because he trusteth in Thee"; and in Psalms, "I will both lay me down in peace and sleep; for Thou, Lord, only makest me dwell in safety."

Every night the old man said the words. And always he found their promise did not fail him.

WEDNESDAY—MAY 24.

NOW, time and time again I've felt,
This surely is the end.
Life's finished, and in grief or shame
I must go round the bend.
A broken heart, a loss, a pain . . .
No sun for me will shine again.

Yet, strange to say, somehow, somehow,
I've plodded on and on,
And found, quite unexpectedly,
That fears or griefs have gone,
For dark and lonely paths have brought
My feet to sunny ways unsought!

THURSDAY—MAY 25.

A READER of this book tells me of an elderly friend who had to be taken to hospital.

Soon after she was admitted she was given a blood transfusion, and a nurse came along to take her pulse.

Of course, since the patient was quite seriously ill, her pulse was so weak the nurse could hardly feel the beat. She looked down at the old soul with a smile, and asked merrily—" Are you living, Granny?"

The old eyes twinkled. " Well," came the reply, " I think I am, but don't take my word for it. Just take hold of my pulse and make sure for yourself!"

FRIDAY—MAY 26.

TICKETS, please!

That's what the ticket-collector called as he opened the door of the compartment. It didn't bother me. I showed him my ticket and sat back.

But the little man facing me searched in vain for his ticket. He got excited and very upset.

In the end he stepped into the corridor and he and the ticket-collector ironed the difficulty out . . . My fellow-passenger had to pay.

Funny thing, a ticket.

If it's the right one, you're equipped for any journey, no matter how far you're going. But if you've no ticket, or if you've the wrong one, you're in for trouble all the way.

And is it not true that this applies not only to a journey by train, bus or plane, but to the journey of life itself?

So to young people who haven't travelled very far along life's road I'd like to say—make sure you've got the right ticket. Otherwise you aren't going to get anywhere.

SATURDAY—MAY 27.

IF you asked me to sum up in the fewest possible words the meaning of religion, I think I should say—" It is faith—that is, believing there is a God and that that God is good."

I am fully aware that for millions today the word FAITH has no meaning at all. They believe only in what they can see or touch.

Faith includes all that—but it goes further. It teaches us to believe where we cannot prove, to trust where we cannot see our way.

SUNDAY—MAY 28.

BEHOLD, I send you forth as sheep in the midst of wolves: be ye therefore wise as serpents, and harmless as doves.

MONDAY—MAY 29.

EPITAPHS are not designed to cheer us, but I came across a French one which seemed to me to be one of the saddest imaginable.

" He was born a man and died a grocer."

Could anything be much sadder than that? Think of it—born a man, with all the possibilities of a man . . . ability to live magnificently, travel, explore, adventure, love and hate, dance and sing, admire and wonder about the stars, climb mountains, laugh and weep and dream . . . and yet, poor fellow, he allowed his world to shrink until long before he died it was scarcely bigger than his coffin. For he worked and lived and thought and bought and sold as a grocer till he became, not a man, but only a money-making machine who had lost his immortal soul.

I must take care that I don't grow smaller with the years.

TUESDAY—MAY 30.

THE Rev. Thomas Jarvie was visiting in his parish some time ago when, quite near his church, he came upon an atheist.

The man was perfectly friendly, but also perfectly frank. He called religion camouflage and he challenged every word Mr Jarvie could say.

Now, you might think a minister would come away from such an encounter with a bitter sense of defeat. But, in fact, Mr Jarvie found himself more stimulated by the man than he could have believed. Against the atheist's attack he had to fight tooth and nail for his own beliefs. And in doing so, his own faith was immeasurably strengthened.

The minister told his congregation about the man. He compared him with those who join the Church as a matter of course, glibly take their vows—then shrug them aside as soon as it suits them.

Then he posed the question—Is it better to be an honest atheist or a dishonest Christian?

It bears thinking about, doesn't it?

WEDNESDAY—MAY 31.

NOTHING'S quite perfect—you know it.
You find, as you travel along,
Whatever your dreams, there is always, it seems,
Just something a little bit wrong . . .
Always a fly in the ointment,
A snag we can't help but lament.

Nothing's quite perfect—consider
There's sunshine to follow the rain,
And after defeat, if you keep on your feet,
There's some little triumph again.
Remember when ready to sigh:
There's always a star in the sky!

JUNE

THURSDAY—JUNE 1.

THIS is the story of a child trapped in the attic of a burning house.

One man in the crowd below held out his arms and shouted to the child to drop from the window. But the child remained where he was.

At last the boy's father came upon the scene. Opening *his* arms, he called—" Jump, Robert, jump!"

Without hesitation, the child jumped to safety.

That's the story.

Don't you think there's a moral here for those of us whose faith is less than it used to be?

Our forefathers had a faith which enabled them to put all their trust in God. Turning to Him, in prayer, they found that hidden source of strength and serenity many of us long for but cannot find.

FRIDAY—JUNE 2.

DID you hear about the crooked nails? It seems that, after the Queen's Coronation, when the seats along the route were being dismantled, one of the foremen joiners noticed a man picking up the rusty, bent six-inch nails which had been left lying about. He asked the man what in the world he wanted them for.

" Where I come from," the man replied, " these would cost a fortune. When I go back home to Tristan da Cunha we will hammer these nails straight and use them again."

The foreman mentioned this to his boss, who told an official, and eventually the story reached the Queen Mother. And that's how two barrels of shining new nails reached lonely Tristan da Cunha, with the Queen Mother's compliments!

SATURDAY—JUNE 3.

FRANCIS GAY is not setting up as a gardening expert. But there is a plant you should never on any account water. It grows fast enough without attention—and if you begin taking care of it, my goodness, it grows so quickly that it shuts out the light, and you find yourself groping in the dark.

I am referring to a plant called grievance. Plant a little grievance in your heart . . . and it will grow big very soon. Begin watering it with your tears, and, goodness me, how it grows.

My advice, for what it's worth, is this—Root out that grievance now. Then plant seeds of kindness or fragrant things which will bring brightness and colour and joy to your heart.

SUNDAY—JUNE 4.

THERE was a man sent from God, whose name was John.

MONDAY—JUNE 5.

THIS little surprise from Ayrshire made my day.

"Dear Francis Gay,—Please use the enclosed £1 as you see fit.

"Last week, I was not looking forward to going through my first driving test. I then read your verse—

'Be strong, my friend, and brave that you
May do the thing you have to do.
Shrink not, though dreading what may be . . .'

"I thought how appropriate it was and I made an inward vow to send you £1 should I pass my test, which I did.

"Your words inspired me and I was brave, though my knees were knocking!"

TUESDAY—JUNE 6.

THERE is a woman who thought life could never be the same for her again.

Her husband had died suddenly and try as she might, she couldn't get over the loss.

Her minister did all he could to console her—but still she was distraught.

Finally he found the answer. He wrote down several addresses on a piece of paper which he handed to the woman. " I'd like you to call on these people," he said, and with a final word of comfort he rose and left her with her grief.

Later, the woman set out to visit the people named on the list, wondering what she would find and why her minister had sent her.

At the first house she found a blind man, desperately in need of a friendly visitor. At the next was an old woman who had lost her husband, and now, in the evening of her days, was cheerless and alone. At another address she met a cripple girl, living gallantly with her disability. And so on; at every house she found someone whose need was greater than her own.

It was the making of the woman, for when she met her minister a few weeks later her tears had gone.

" I've found," she said, " that in helping others to carry their cross, mine is easier to bear."

WEDNESDAY—JUNE 7.

LORD, bless the folk who pray and serve—
And likewise those who don't;
For all the folk—the good and bad,
Including even me—
Have in them secret strength and grace
To live as pleases Thee!

THURSDAY—JUNE 8.

I DON'T know when I enjoyed a church service more. The Lady of the House and I set out aiming for nowhere in particular and found ourselves in Pitlochry on the Saturday evening. Next morning we strolled leisurely along to the little country church of Moulin in time for the service.

I think half of the congregation were visitors, like ourselves.

But, my, how we all sang, "Pleasant are Thy courts above . . . pleasant are Thy courts below." It seemed the whole congregation were doing their best to send the song straight to heaven!

Full marks to Moulin for singing which made you thrill to the very gladness in it!

FRIDAY—JUNE 9.

DO you remember that little story of the nurse who was doing her bit in a London hospital during the last war?

The German raids were hotting up considerably, and night after night, fire fell from heaven.

From the West of England her father sent her a telegram—"Pack bag and come home at once."

A few hours later he received a telegram which said—"Sorry. No bag to pack. Not coming."

That second telegram had been sent off after one of the worst raids ever. The hospital had been badly hit, and the little nurse had lost everything except the clothes she was wearing.

But she didn't quit.

Why serve up an old war story after all these years? Simply because it may be that you have a job on hand which threatens to get you down.

Of course, you *could* down tools and run away . . . but, like the nurse, I bet you won't!

SATURDAY—JUNE 10.

AT a Sunday school picnic a boy of eight or nine was running far behind the others in a race.

When the others had finished he was still determined to reach the tape. So much so that those watching him could see his lips moving silently.

Soon afterwards he did puff past the tape, and the minister asked him what he had been saying. "Oh, I was praying," answered the laddie. "Not to *win* the race, but just to finish. You see, I asked God to pick my feet up—and I'd put them down."

Just another way of saying God helps those who help themselves.

SUNDAY—JUNE 11.

AND as they thus spake, Jesus Himself stood in the midst of them, and saith unto them, Peace be unto you.

MONDAY—JUNE 12.

EVERY night at eight o'clock the bells of Brixham Church peal out a verse of "Abide With Me."

A friend told me how deeply impressed he was at this tribute to Henry Francis Lyte, who wrote the wonderful hymn.

You see, Henry Francis Lyte was vicar of the tiny fishing community at Brixham, on the Devon coast.

Now a great church stands there to his memory.

It is a noble memorial. Its carillon of bells was paid for by people all over the world.

Come to think of it, when you unite the bells of Brixham with the singing of "Abide With Me" in our churches every other Sunday—what a massive tribute we all pay to the man who gave us our lovely evening prayer.

TUESDAY—JUNE 13.

IT'S wonderful what can be done with a kindly thought—and an old deckchair!

Mrs Loxam bought the chair second-hand at the beginning of the summer. Each day she carried it outside and set it up on the sunny side of the square opposite her house. And each evening she folded the chair up and took it home again.

But don't imagine Mrs Loxam sat all day sunning herself. It was for anyone in the square to sit in and enjoy the sunshine!

All the thanks she asked was that those who sat in the chair should put a penny in the little box beside it. You see, Mrs Loxam is great-aunt to a boy who has been in a home for spastics for five years. Everyone has been so kind to him there, she wondered what she could do to show her gratitude.

Her second-hand deckchair brought in 8s 6d in pennies, and with 1s 6d of her own, she sent off the money to the hospital for her good cause.

Maybe 10s doesn't seem much—but I doubt if it has ever been earned with more earnestness.

WEDNESDAY—JUNE 14.

UP there at my garden
I lean upon my spade,
And talk to John or Andrew
While glowing sunsets fade.
I'll maybe lend my fellow man
A garden fork or watering-can.
A friendly crack is pleasant—
It makes the spirit grow;
I ask advice of Andrew
Or tell John what I know.
And now and then I'll do a spot
Of weeding in my little plot!

THURSDAY—JUNE 15.

"DEAR Francis Gay—After a brilliant day, the sun was dipping below the horizon.

"The swish of the bows slicing through the placid waters of the Bay of Biscay allowed no other sound to reach us . . . it was all so peaceful.

"Said my friend, who does social work in the Midlands of England—'In a moment like this, when the world is being so kind to you and me, it is difficult to believe it can be so ruthlessly hard to so many.'

"Then she told me about the little boy she visited before sailing.

"His father was unknown, but he was coloured. The boy had been abandoned by his mother. And, just after being accepted into the care of a welfare haven, he had contracted polio.

"'As I looked down at that helpless, crippled little mite, so alone in the world, my heart bled for him. Why should so much misfortune have to be shouldered by one so tiny being?' . . ."

FRIDAY—JUNE 16.

HAVE you ever thought things out this way?

Nine times out of ten, when a big trouble smashes into our lives, we have the courage and strength and grace to carry on magnificently. What so often gets us down is not the big burden, but the small, yet constant, irritation.

Isn't it true that so often the housewife has a nervous breakdown just because every day is harassing, so many things vex her, the sheer monotony gets on her nerves?

That's why I think every woman in the home needs to offer a little daily prayer—"Lord, give me grace and patience to smile my way through the hours from getting up to going to bed."

SATURDAY—JUNE 17.

THE other day, someone asked me to define joy, or happiness.

It made me think, I can tell you, until I remembered a few words I read or heard somewhere. The origin of them I have forgotten, but the words themselves I shall never forget:—

" Happiness is the flag we fly when the King has taken up residence in our hearts."

It's a wonderful description, isn't it? For surely happiness shines in our faces, and in our smiles, just as a flag flies proudly for all to see. There may be times when it's at half-mast—but it's still there.

So remember—at all costs, keep the flag flying!

SUNDAY—JUNE 18.

AND of His fulness have all we received, and grace for grace.

MONDAY—JUNE 19.

BETWEEN three and four o'clock on a Friday is the magic hour for an old lady in Loanhead.

She is a patient in hospital there, and she is blind and has lost her legs.

But every Friday one of the Woman's Guild visits her. It's not that there's anything very exceptional in the short hour they have together. Why, the visitor just sits by the old lady's bedside and reads to her from a magazine.

Then she tells what is going on in the town, all the little changes which the blind lady can picture in her mind's eye.

As I say, it's just a wee thing, but it's gone on faithfully every Friday for years, and to me it is the very essence of God's work here below.

TUESDAY—JUNE 20.

REV. FRANK FOXON was a Naval chaplain at Rosyth. It was there he met a man who had sunk to rock bottom . . . a young sailor caught up in a life of drunken sordidness, gambling, thieving.

Mr Foxon pleaded with him, argued with him, prayed for him. But the sailor only sneered.

One day he was posted and, as a last attempt to influence him, Mr Foxon gave him a New Testament with a copy of the 23rd Psalm rewritten specially for sailors. Perhaps you know the one. It begins " The Lord is my Pilot. I shall not drift . . ."

Months passed, years wore on. Mr Foxon moved from Rosyth to England, then to Clydebank.

One morning the postman handed him a letter. Mr Foxon opened it. Yes, it was a message from the sailor and it said simply—" I'm sorry for all the trouble I caused you, Padre. It's all right now. *He* is my Pilot."

Can you wonder that these words are perhaps the happiest Mr Foxon has ever read?

WEDNESDAY—JUNE 21.

WE walked a mile in heaven's courts
An hour after tea—
Just up the lane, across the fields,
Our little Pete and me.

Oh, how he prattled on and on,
And made a daisy chain;
Then talked of sweet and lovely things
Again and yet again.

His hand in mine, we wandered home,
Myself and little Pete;
I wish my thoughts were pure, like his,
My spirit half as sweet.

THURSDAY—JUNE 22.

ONE of the great religious figures in Scotland last century was Robert Rainy, at one time Principal of New College, Edinburgh.

The doctor was a learned man—but learning did not make him long-faced. It seems that nothing ever robbed him of his kindly disposition and natural cheeriness.

Principal Rainy had an unconquerable faith—perhaps that was his secret.

His day, of course, was different from our own, and you and I have worries which he never knew. But it does appear to be beyond all argument that the true Christian has within him a well-spring of joy which nothing can ever dry up. Underneath all the vexation and apprehensions which are his he *knows* that God is love, and that all *must* be well!

FRIDAY—JUNE 23.

IF ever you feel that the light has gone out of your life, I beg of you to think of Mrs Beattie.

There she was, an elderly woman—alone, blind and almost helpless. Nothing could be more pathetic.

One day, she went into hospital for an operation on one eye. The doctors didn't hold out much hope and, alas, the operation was not a success.

Undaunted, Mrs Beattie about a year later went in for an operation on the other eye. Again there was only a faint chance, but, when it was all over, she could see almost as well as she had ever done.

Miraculously Mrs Beattie's darkness has been banished, she has handed back her blind pension and today she is living a full and happy life again.

So, if life ever seems to be black for you and the future seems to hold no hope—think of Mrs Beattie and the courage and faith that brought her through.

SATURDAY—JUNE 24.

I WAS speaking with a minister who has two jobs. One is to see to the running of his own church. The other is visiting a home for mentally-ill patients.

Here's what he was telling me—"The amazing thing is so many of the people there ought not, you would think, to be there at all.

"When I ask them questions, they reply sensibly enough. They say they had no money troubles. They weren't worn out or frightened or killed with work. They were very fortunate people, as it appeared, who had only one trouble—*Too much time to think about themselves!*"

SUNDAY—JUNE 25.

TRULY my soul waiteth upon God: from Him cometh my salvation.

MONDAY—JUNE 26.

THESE verses were sent to me by a prisoner in Peterhead Prison—

I have always taken for granted
The good things on this earth,
But never stopped to value
Their presence or their worth.

The babbling brook, the green-leafed tree,
The fields, the flowers, the buzzing bee;
These beautiful sights seem far away
Now that time is my enemy.

But I think of them now as in a dream,
And I long for the day when I am free,
God's wonderful gifts once more I will see,
When time is no longer my enemy.

TUESDAY—JUNE 27.

ONE day a doctor's prescription was handed in to a busy chemist's shop in Glasgow.

" Come back in an hour," said the chemist, with scarce a glance at his customer.

" Dear me," said the customer, the Rev. Robert Ferguson, " that shouldn't take more than five minutes . . ."

And, would you believe it, before five minutes were up Mr Ferguson not only had his prescription—but also a job making up prescriptions during staff holidays !

You see, what the busy chemist could not know at first was that Mr Ferguson qualified as a pharmacist before he was a minister. And luckily for the chemist, Mr Ferguson was on pulpit supply and had time to spare while he was waiting for a church of his own.

Before long, Mr Ferguson was measuring and dispensing with his old skill. Indeed, he was such a success he was moved to Glasgow Eye Infirmary and then to Glasgow Western Infirmary. He might even have kept on, for he was offered an important post as a pharmacist.

But he turned it down. Why? Because his heart lay in the service where healing is a calling that needs no medicine, but faith . . .

WEDNESDAY—JUNE 28.

SCISSORS held by wrinkled hands,
In her garden there she stands . . .
Snip, snip, snip—the sweetpeas drop;
Little old lady, why not stop !
A rainbow bunch of sweetness she
Gives, with a lovely smile, to me.
" I like sweetpeas," I hear her say.
" I grow them just to give away !"

TO A YOUNG PHOTOGRAPHER

Now daffodils are out again
Along the waterside,
And I hope you'll get a photograph
To show around with pride.
And richer still, a memory
To store away inside.

David Hope

LIFE'S VOYAGE

Sometimes like these boats am I :
Out of water, high and dry.
Yet I doubt not from His main
Tides of faith will flood again,
And then refreshed I'll venture out
And safely cross life's sea of doubt.

DAVID HOPE

Thursday—June 29.

I AM thinking of the pact that Commandos made before battle. It was simply, " I'll stand by your folk if you stand by mine."

Then, with that promise made, they went forward into the unknown. As often as not the words were unspoken, but each knew, from the strength of their comradeship, that his mates would look after his loved ones . . .

And so it has been.

How true to the spirit of the Commandos, whose courage, selflessness, aye, and compassion, were never greater than when things were at their worst.

Maybe we could do well to remember them—and their pact—when, at times, living is so often a case of, " I'm all right."

Friday—June 30.

SAMMY worked at the local power station until he was 65 and had to retire. But for an active man like him, doing nothing was unthinkable, so he looked about—and found himself a job to his liking.

He decided to take two men for a walk every day!

They are Willie, the shepherd, and Bob, the ploughman, and both have lost their sight.

Now he's given them a new lease of life. Every day, rain or shine, he has called and taken them out along the country roads they both knew so well.

If you were near enough, you could hear Sammy giving his friends the news. Their ears are tuned to the country sounds, and he supplies the eyes.

Words alone can't tell what all this means to the two blind men. But if you ever feel a thrill as you walk in the warmth of a summer's eve, watching the breeze spread silver ripples over the old mill dam, then you may have an inkling . . . .

JULY

SATURDAY—JULY 1.

AN elderly Glasgow couple went to Scarborough for their holiday. They had never been there before and they felt just a wee bit "lost".

But what a surprise they had when they entered the dining-room. They were directed to a table which stood out from all the others because on it stood a beautiful vase of flowers, with a card saying, "Welcome to Scarborough. I have ordered the sunshine for you.—Love, Bert."

The flowers had been ordered by the couple's son in New Zealand and the joy they gave could hardly have been greater if the son had been there to welcome the old folk himself.

SUNDAY—JULY 2.

I AM that bread of life.

MONDAY—JULY 3.

A FRIEND of mine was talking about his student days the other evening.

"We were always in a hurry. We could never get anything done quickly enough."

He went on to tell me how once they'd jumped off a train at the station, dashed down the platform and pelted down the street to catch a bus by the skin of their teeth.

"Fine," my friend had gasped as he sank back in his seat. "We've saved three minutes."

"Yes," said one of their number, "we've saved three minutes. And now that we've got them, what are we going to do with them?"

Makes you think, doesn't it?

TUESDAY—JULY 4.

FOR more than 50 years old Nell didn't have a friend in the world.

There was, of course, the devoted staff of the big mental hospital near Epsom, where Nell lived out her life. They cared for her well. But can you imagine what it must have meant to her in all these years never to have a visitor, and never to go out with someone she could call her own?

Old Nell was over 90 when she died. When she went to the crematorium there was no mourner and no service. She passed on as alone and forgotten as she had lived.

It is one of the saddest things I have ever heard. Yet what is even sadder is that it is far from the whole story. In two miles around Epsom there are five mental hospitals, and in them are nearly 2500 folk who, like old Nell, are without a friend.

I am thankful to add that recently a League of Friends has been formed to visit such forgotten souls and bring them companionship.

It is a mighty and challenging task. I'm sure they have God's grace in its doing.

WEDNESDAY—JULY 5.

JUST a picture postcard
Sent by Auntie Dot.
"All my love; will see you soon,
Thinking of you in Dunoon!"

Who can say what pleasure
That one postcard gave
To a cripple laddie,
Lonely, weak—yet brave?
Nice to know folk think of you—
Nice to get a line or two!

THURSDAY—JULY 6.

THREE cheers for the eleven salesmen in Glasgow! They took a day off and went to the coast in their cars. But not alone.

From an old people's home they picked up seven surprised passengers. The Guild of Aid in the Gorbals, promptly supplied another 23.

The old folk had a slap-up lunch at Largs, where they visited friends or just sat in the sunshine enjoying a gossip. Then a grand high tea, and in the gloaming the cars turned for home.

It was difficult to know who enjoyed the day most—the old folk or the salesmen who supplied their own cars, paid for everything, and gave up their day's work to do so.

We're inclined to think of salesmen only as very practical businessmen. No doubt they are, but I know eleven of them who are more than that.

FRIDAY—JULY 7.

CAN you imagine washing your face with your breath? Unreal, you say? And yet, my friends, during the long years of the war it was as real to the men of the submarines as life itself.

At sea, every man was their enemy. Only the night was their friend—for only then could they breathe the open air.

Once submerged, they lived and slept at their posts. Their breath condensed on the steel plates and ran off into a tank. In that they washed.

When hunted, they took off their sandals lest the least tremor of sound should reach the enemy and betray them. And when attacked, there was nowhere to run to, no one to call to for help.

We can only imagine what these men endured. But we should remember they endured it for us.

SATURDAY—JULY 8.

A FEW days ago a friend of mine handed me this little item, with the query—"Say, Francis, what kind of Christian are *you*?"

It seems that a lot of Christians are like wheelbarrows—no use unless pushed.

Some are like kites—if you don't keep a string on them they fly away.

Some are like kittens—most contented when petted.

Some are like balloons—full of their own importance and ready to blow up.

Some are like trailers—they have to be pulled.

Some, fortunately, are like a good watch—open-faced, pure gold, quietly busy and full of good works.

SUNDAY—JULY 9.

A MAN that hath friends must shew himself friendly: and there is a Friend that sticketh closer than a brother.

MONDAY—JULY 10.

I SAW it the other evening on the battlefield of Culloden Moor. My eye was caught by something fluttering in the breeze from one of the weathered headstones.

There, lying across the top of the Mackintosh stone, lay a scrap of clan tartan.

It had obviously been cut from the kilt of a visitor and it was as splendid as a banner unfurled.

I do not know who put it there. Neither, I suppose, did the countless visitors who gazed on it, as we did.

But we agreed that no Highland hero could wish for a prouder epitaph than the tartan he wore and served and loved.

TUESDAY—JULY 11.

I'M sorry that my friends, somehow,
Do stupid things, or say
The very silliest of things
Quite often every day.
I shake my head, and sigh a bit,
Such foolishness to see . . .
And only hope my many friends
Don't think the same of me!

WEDNESDAY—JULY 12.

EVERY morning John Drummond shaves the wrong way round. He doesn't move his hand—he moves his face.

His razor is fixed in a long metal tube. He holds the end of the tube with both hands, then carefully draws his face and chin across the edge of the blade.

It is a slow, laborious operation, symbolic of the courage and patience of a man who has borne much and refuses to give in.

John was born with hands, legs and ankles twisted in such a way it was impossible to use them normally. For years he underwent treatment and endured great pain, as surgeons gradually straightened his limbs and joints.

When the operations were over he had to learn, literally, to stand on his own feet and make his own way. He had to learn to walk, to dress himself, to fix his shoes, even to comb his hair, which he did for the first time when he was 26. And, above all, he had to learn a job. It's almost incredible, I know, but John has done all these things.

John will always be crippled to some extent, of course. But as I picture him this morning, busy with his razor, I marvel that sheer determination can accomplish so much.

THURSDAY—JULY 13.

MRS CHILDS is a pensioner.

Her wee house was the only one in the building still with gas light. For years it served her well. Then, unaccountably, she became rather nervous of it and feared what might happen if the flame accidentally went out. So to be on the safe side she used the gas less and less, even for cooking.

Then one day, out of the blue, a young captain from the Salvation Army called—and discovered Mrs Childs' fear. Before you could say General Booth, she got an electrician to put in electric light for Mrs Childs, including a light at her bed.

You ought to see what a bright wee home Mrs Childs has now. No wonder she says "God bless the captain." And I say it too!

FRIDAY—JULY 14.

WHAT, I wonder, will we cherish most when we grow old. Mr Alex. Logan tells me of one of his proudest moments.

"When I was scarcely ten years old," he writes, "I drew my first pay packet as a half-timer in the local flax mill—3s 3d for a fortnight.

"Proudly I ran out of the mill gate, then along the High Street, with my pay clutched tightly in my hand. I never stopped running until I arrived home.

"Mother was resting in her old armchair when I rushed up to her and laid my pay packet on her lap.

"With a fond smile, she kissed me, and said the words I will never forget as long as I live. 'Oh, my wee laddie's a man now, and a bread-winner. I'm proud o' my wee son.'

"In my old age I cherish many happy memories of my long life, but my mother's kiss and her words of praise that day are the most vivid of them all."

SATURDAY—JULY 15.

I HEARD about an old farmer who was never quite satisfied with anything.

The weather was always "too dry," or "too wet," and when the sun and the rain *did* come, they apparently arrived at the wrong time.

But one year the weather was as near perfect as anyone could expect. Every farmer had a bumper crop, and when the harvest was in, they all relaxed and smiled. All except one—the old man who groused.

"Oh, aye," he was forced to admit to his neighbour, "it's a grand crop all right." Then his brow furrowed. "But did you ever think how much a crop like that takes out of the ground?"

Yes, if you look for a cloud you can usually find one, even on the brightest day.

Fortunately, the reverse is true too. Even when the sky is grey, there's sure to be a patch of sunshine somewhere—and that's *really* worth looking for!

SUNDAY—JULY 16.

JESUS stood and cried, saying, If any man thirst, let him come unto Me, and drink.

MONDAY—JULY 17.

A FRIEND tells me that very recently he was harassed by financial matters and terribly anxious about his wife's health. Things are fine now—but while it lasted it was a dreadful thing, going to work with a great weight on the shoulders, a kind of blackness in the mind.

"Only one thing enabled me to keep going," he told me. "The knowledge that either all would be well or that God would give me strength to endure if the worst happened."

THE WAY OF A GULL

When the gulls come down for breakfast
Do they smile or anything,
That we, poor Lords of Nature,
Can't even flap a wing?

DAVID HOPE

A SUMMER DAY

Memory's like a fisher's net—
This remember, this forget.
But I give thanks for little things
That the net so often brings.
A glimpse of sunshine long ago,
A shore where warm sea breezes blow,

Placid horses cropping grass,
Idly watching as I pass—
Earth and sea and sky all blent
In one moment of content.
I gazed and gazed and went my way,
The richer by a summer day.

David Hope

THE VIGIL *

Where every stone recalls
Men great in a nation's story,
He takes the ancient vow—
" For others—not for glory."

DAVID HOPE

* Ritual associated with the introduction of a Rover Scout into a crew.

TUESDAY—JULY 18.

MRS McINTOSH loved children dearly, but, alas, her husband was killed in the war.

It was then that Mrs McIntosh filled the yearning in her heart by helping the very children who most needed love and care. She became the first woman visitor in the Scottish Society for the Prevention of Cruelty to Children.

In her first case she found three little children running unwashed and barefoot on a bare floor. The whole family slept in one bed. There wasn't a bite of food in the house.

The mother had lost heart. Her husband was in prison. The rent wasn't paid.

Oh, it would have been so easy for Mrs McIntosh to be angry and criticise. Instead, in sheer compassion, she took the family to her heart.

And do you know the first thing she did? She gave the mother a bath-cube and packed her off for a bath. If ever wonders began with a bath-cube, they began then.

Today, the family has a nice, clean home. They're out of debt. The father is working and there's happiness and respect where once there was only despair.

And, miraculously, it all began with Mrs McIntosh's own unhappiness.

WEDNESDAY—JULY 19.

BE strong, my friend, and brave that you
May do the things you have to do.
Shrink not. Though dreading what may be,
Your conscience clear, your spirit free,
How glad you'll feel to think delay
And hesitance are done away,
When once what now must be begun
Is splendidly and rightly done.

THURSDAY—JULY 20.

IT'S a disturbing yet challenging thought that in spite of all the advances of science there are still a lot of really hungry people in the world.

Just how many there are, neither you nor I can have even the faintest idea . . . but if they stood in a straight line from your door, each man, woman or child two feet apart, the line would go round the world 25 times . . . and because of the increase in population, it's increasing 20 miles a day!

Americans are criticised for this and that, but I take off my hat to church-going people of that great country, for they are raising something like 12 million dollars a year to help the desperately needy.

It's an impressive record by any standards . . . and we in this country have already done much along these lines. But perhaps we might do even more.

FRIDAY—JULY 21.

RECENTLY I visited Grace McNaught. She was so bonnie she looked more like a schoolgirl than a young woman of 29 who has been practically a prisoner in her bed for eight years.

It all began with a small arthritic pain near the back of her neck. In time, she had to give up her job, dancing, swimming, tennis.

Today Grace cannot stand up or sit down unaided. She has to be lifted up and down the step at the door to sit a while in the garden. She told me without a quiver that she will never be any better . . .

I marvelled at the strength and brightness of so young a spirit. You might think that Grace has precious little to look forward to, yet I can tell you she hasn't an ounce of self-pity.

I don't really know if my visit helped her. But I do know she helped me.

SATURDAY—JULY 22.

MANY years ago an old lady in Westmorland used to hold evening Bible classes for young girls of the district.

Ah, you may say, that was many years ago. It couldn't happen now.

But, my friend, that's where you'd be wrong. For in the village of Dunshelt it *is* happening—and the kindly soul who has organised it is one of the girls who enjoyed the evenings in Westmorland.

To her house come about 15 young girls who sing hymns and have Bible readings and stories, just as Mrs Scott and her friends did many years ago.

While a story is being read, the other girls sew or knit for a mission home or charity.

Isn't it marvellous how the kindly action of an old Westmorland woman many years ago has blossomed in a way she never dreamed of?

SUNDAY—JULY 23.

VERILY, verily, I say unto you, he that heareth My word, and believeth on Him that sent Me, hath everlasting life, and shall not come into condemnation; but is passed from death unto life.

MONDAY—JULY 24.

I LIKE this story of an old farmer who was asked which church he belonged to.

He thought for a moment, then looked at his friend.

"Every week I go to market," he said slowly. "There are quite a few roads I can take to get there.

"But when I arrive at the market, they don't ask me which road I came by. They only ask me if my corn is good . . ."

TUESDAY—JULY 25.

CAN you mix with other men?
How I hope you can
Mingle with a jolly crowd,
Be a friendly man.
But dare you be alone sometimes,
Only sea and sky
Sharing secrets of your heart
While the minutes fly?
O, how green the mountain sod
When you walk alone with God!

WEDNESDAY—JULY 26.

I WONDER if faith has ever been a surer shield than to Keith McWilliam?

Ever since he was a boy, Keith wanted to be a minister. And with all the glowing certainty of youth, he *knew* he would be some day.

When the First World War broke out he was still a student at Aberdeen University, but he joined the Gordons and marched off as a private soldier to Flanders. And through all that dreadful war, Keith *knew* he would come back to serve God.

Once he was in a platoon moving up to the front line at Armentieres. A shell landed among them. Blast and fumes filled the air, and when his head and eyes cleared, he saw 14 kilted comrades lying dead. Yet he himself was unscathed, and wonderful to relate, he remained unscathed when, time after time death came just as close.

Yes, Keith McWilliam kept faith with his faith. He became a minister after the war and has been one for nearly 40 years.

Now he is retired and lives in Hamilton, and I know he still acknowledges the Hand that so surely set him aside for a chosen task all these years ago.

THURSDAY—JULY 27.

NEVER say—" This is the end." Every end is also a new beginning.

Never try to appear cleverer or richer or more important than you are—you can't fool people.

Never be sorry for yourself more than five minutes —start counting your blessings instead.

Never think it's no good trying to do something—you *can* do it with patience and determination.

Never be ashamed of owning that you were in the wrong—even the best people err at times.

Never try to get your own back—that's being even worse than the other party.

Never lose your faith in God.

Never miss an opportunity of helping somebody.

Never be afraid to start all over again.

FRIDAY—JULY 28.

HAWTHORNBRAE Children's Home at Duddingston was the only home the girl had ever known. She left when she was 15 to start work. Then she fell in love with a young man and he asked her to marry him.

Before the girl gave her answer, she asked the advice of Mrs Moore, the matron of the home.

Then came a letter from the girl, asking if she and her husband could spend their honeymoon at Hawthornbrae. Mrs Moore wrote back at once, saying she'd be delighted.

When the young couple arrived they found Mrs Moore and all her " family " of 35 children waiting on the steps to greet them.

I'm told Mrs Moore's smile was the happiest, and I think I know why—for the girl who came to spend her honeymoon had shown that to her Hawthornbrae was not just a Home—but truly a home.

SATURDAY—JULY 29.

A FRIEND writes to tell me that it has taken him eight years to get his small garden to his liking, and that now, at last, he's going to sit in a deck-chair and look at it and enjoy it.

"No sense," he tells me in his delightful letter, "in digging and weeding and toiling and moiling just so that the neighbours may look over the wall and admire my herbaceous borders and my impeccable lawn. I'm now going to do nothing in the large manner; and if anybody finds fault with me I'll quote Sir Alan Herbert, and say in a jingling tone:

"Let's stop somebody doing something!
Everybody's doing too much!"

SUNDAY—JULY 30.

AND the next day John seeth Jesus coming unto him, and saith, Behold the Lamb of God, which taketh away the sin of the world.

MONDAY—JULY 31.

IT could only happen in Sunday school!

After a talk on the Nativity and the Flight to Egypt, the children were asked to make a drawing of the scene.

One little lad drew a picture of Mary and Joseph and the baby Jesus—in an aeroplane. The teacher of course, was puzzled and asked the laddie to explain.

Right away, he said—"Well, Joseph and Mary were flying to Egypt."

"Yes, but who is that sitting in front of them?" he was asked.

"Oh," said the wee lad, "that's Pontius, the pilot!"

AUGUST

TUESDAY—AUGUST 1.

ERIC DELVES was wounded badly in the R.A.F. during the war, and after years in hospital he went home broken in health and spirit, unfit to work . . . and perhaps to die.

Then those splendid folk, the War Disabled Help Department of the Red Cross, suggested he might like a little greenhouse to give him an interest. Eric had never really thought about it and, more not to seem ungrateful than anything else, he thanked them for their offer, and accepted it.

As Eric Delves worked away, half-heartedly at first, beauty grew and flourished under his hands and something within him changed. He began to enjoy the hours spent in its warmth and greenness, and, what's more, his health improved.

Now, believe it or not, the man who felt he had come home to die has won a collection of prizes, cups and medals—and a new, bigger greenhouse for growing produce.

So if, by chance, you feel that life holds little for you, and the prospect before you seems hopeless, think of Eric Delves and of the greenhouse that worked wonders for him.

WEDNESDAY—AUGUST 2.

IF you can take a good brisk walk
And not get out of puff,
If you can do the things you want
Because you've strength enough—
Be glad and humble you are fit,
That life for you is good . . .
And think about the folk who'd do
As you do if they could !

THURSDAY—AUGUST 3.

I HEARD recently of a man who is in prison. It seems that for a time now he has been interested in spastic children, and he wanted to help them in some way.

Perhaps you might say to yourself, there isn't much a man can do locked away in prison. That's where you would be wrong, for this prisoner is building —of all things—model yachts!

And I must explain these are no ordinary models. He has a wide knowledge of the real thing. So his yachts aren't toys, but scale models, perfect in every detail and up to six feet long! How he manages to build them in prison is a mystery to me.

As a prisoner, he earns only 5s 10d a week, yet he wants to give his yachts away. He feels that if they can raise money to bring happiness to spastic children, his days in prison will not have been wasted.

FRIDAY—AUGUST 4.

AN ordinary penny!

When we visited the hydro-electric station at Pitlochry we saw it, balanced on its edge on top of one of the generators. The penny stands there all the time, for the great generator is so accurately made and so smooth in its running that there isn't even enough vibration to knock the coin over.

All round is the hum of the generators and the crashing of the rushing water—yet in the midst of it all is this motionless penny.

It's rather like life, isn't it? There are times when the hustle and bustle of our daily routine tend to get us down, and we feel we can no longer keep up the pace. When you feel like that — remember the penny.

For if we can find that inner stillness we'll be able to stand upright just like the penny of Pitlochry.

MORNING PAPERS

How are things in London town,
What's our M.P. saying?
Are my shares going up or down?
How are Rangers playing?

Bargains, bargains all the way,
From grocers and from drapers,
I wouldn't like to start the day
Without the morning papers.

DAVID HOPE

THE WAY WE GO

Easier the hills we climb,
Brighter smiles the weather,
Happier the journey when
Friends travel it together.

DAVID HOPE

SATURDAY—AUGUST 5.

A WIDOW who lost her only son not very long ago has an understanding with her grocer that every week he supplies a really good selection of goods to a poor family—and sends her the bill.

When the grocer asked why she was doing this lovely thing she replied: "Because it's better to light one little candle than to curse the darkness."

SUNDAY—AUGUST 6.

BEHOLD, God is my salvation; I will trust, and not be afraid: for the Lord Jehovah is my strength and my song; He also is become my salvation.

MONDAY—AUGUST 7.

I WONDER if any woman makes more—or better—jam than the Lady of the House.

We were busy at it together, her ladyship and I.

The big copper jelly pan was bright and shining. The berries, plump and firm, lay measured out inside it. The sugar stood by, ready at a moment's notice.

Soon the wonderful smell of boiling strawberry jam wisped through the kitchen and the rows of shining jars were filled up.

When she's finished, a whole big cupboard is crammed full—rows and rows of jars.

Where it all goes, I don't know. Some stays at home, of course. A lot goes to the sale of work. Some mysteriously disappears at Christmas. And I know that whenever her ladyship visits one of her old bodies, there's normally a jar in her bag for them.

So the annual wonder of seed time and harvest has begun, and somehow it makes me feel good that in countless homes the womenfolk already have something in store for the harsh winter days ahead.

TUESDAY—AUGUST 8.

I AM sure it will always be a golden moment in the life of the Rev. Brian Kingsmore.

One Sunday evening in Park Congregational Church, Airdrie, Mr Kingsmore preached his first sermon as a minister.

After pronouncing the Benediction, Mr Kingsmore sat down and bent his head in prayer.

Softly, the choir began to sing their vesper, " Abide With Me," and as the beautiful old hymn rose through the still air of the church, a strange and beautiful thing happened.

Someone in the congregation joined in the singing. Then another, and another.

In a trice, the whole church was singing with all their hearts. For on this occasion it wasn't just a vesper, or even a hymn. It was a prayer from every soul there for the young man who had become their minister, and who was starting out anew on the way God had set before him.

I can't think of a lovelier prayer—

" When other helpers fail and comforts flee,
Help of the helpless, O, abide with me . . ."

And I'm sure that in the years ahead, if ever the road seems a little rough for Mr Kingsmore, he will remember that first Sunday evening, and draw strength and courage from the prayer that was offered for him so spontaneously.

WEDNESDAY—AUGUST 9.

NOW for the bucket and spade once again,
Now for the grouse on the moor,
Now for a cruise or a fortnight in France,
Now for a mystery tour . . .
Holidays, holidays—thrilling to roam;
Almost as thrilling as coming back home!

THURSDAY—AUGUST 10.

IT seems that an American divinity student at St Andrews was fascinated by the Lammas Fair in the town. It's a wonderful street fair—with side-shows, stalls and all sorts of attractions.

Then the American thought to himself—" I wonder if the children in St David's Home will be seeing this?" You see, St David's is where children from broken homes find their feet again. And although the Matron and her staff do their best, the bairns do miss some things.

And the upshot was that four wide-eyed laddies found themselves sampling all the fun of the fair—the roundabouts, shooting galleries, hoop-la and hosts of other exciting things—with a new friend who simply appeared from out of the blue.

Thank you, Mr American, I'm proud of you.

FRIDAY—AUGUST 11.

A FRIEND of mine in Newcastle visited a home for incurables some years ago.

He had been asked to conduct a service in a ward where 30 elderly women lay bedridden.

My friend recalls that just as he entered the ward he slipped on the polished floor, and he skidded half-way across the room to the sound of startled " Ohs!"

It was not the happiest way of beginning a service but he went bravely on. " My dear friends," he began, " I would rather you chose the hymns, as I am sure you have your favourites. Any suggestions for our opening hymn?"

Instantly some quavering voices called for, " Stand Up, Stand Up For Jesus!" Then the whole ward rocked with laughter.

If there isn't a challenge in all this for you and me, I'm a Dutchman.

SATURDAY—AUGUST 12.

THE stranger had no magic wand, I know, but to the Burris family she was a real fairy godmother.

Mrs Burris decided to take her three youngest children on a camping holiday.

It was a hard thing for her to do, because at Christmas her husband died and this was to be the first holiday the children would have without their daddy.

The family found a lovely camping spot down the Clyde—but after five glorious days, the rain came and didn't stop until even the matches in the tents were soaked.

So with Jimmy, a wee man of ten, Mrs Burris set out to find shelter. At last, they came to a big house on the estate, and a gracious lady answered their knock. She listened to their story—and took charge of everything.

First, she drove to the waterlogged camp. Next she uprooted the tents, bundled everything and everyone into her car, and drove them to a little dream cottage, with a pile of firewood specially brought for them.

Need I say that the rest of their holiday was like a fairy tale.

I wish I could tell you the name of the lady who made it all possible. Instead, I add my thanks to a total stranger who stepped in and saved the holiday for a whole family.

SUNDAY—AUGUST 13.

COME unto Me, all ye that labour and are heavy laden, and I will give you rest. Take My yoke upon you, and learn of Me; for I am meek and lowly in heart: and ye shall find rest unto your souls. For My yoke is easy, and My burden is light.

MONDAY—AUGUST 14.

THE Lady of the House laughed when I told her this.

It's said that General Mark Clark, the great American soldier, was once asked what was the best advice he had ever been given in the course of his career.

" Oh," said the general. " There's no doubt about that. It was the suggestion that I should marry the girl who is now my wife!"

The questioner pressed on. " And who was it," he said, " who advised you to marry her?"

A smile crossed the General's face. " Funnily enough," he replied, " it was my wife herself!"

TUESDAY—AUGUST 15.

HOW often, I wonder, do you visit a hospital bed? Once or twice a year, maybe, to see one of the family or a friend?

Well, here's somebody who visits not two or three times a year—but a thousand patients *every week!*

That is the splendid record of Mrs Arthur.

She's in her seventies now, and can't get about as well as she used to, but, bless her, she tries to visit every hospital bed in Aberdeen every week.

She doesn't pause long at each bed—just long enough to smile and greet each patient with an encouraging message and a quiet word. Sometimes she is the only visitor a patient has for weeks on end.

When did Mrs Arthur begin her labour of love? Believe it or not, it was when she was a lassie in her twenties, about 50 years ago. And she's been doing it ever since, though the task grows ever more difficult as the number of sick folk in hospital increases.

I doubt if many of Mrs Arthur's patients could tell you her name, yet I know that no one who has been in hospital in Aberdeen will ever forget her.

WEDNESDAY—AUGUST 16.

LOTS and lots of things to do—
Easy to get fussed;
This and that all in a rush—
'Ware that you don't bust!
Dashing here and there all day,
All your patience gone . . .
Why not just ease up a bit?
DO THINGS ONE BY ONE!

THURSDAY—AUGUST 17.

WILLIE ANNAN'S house was just opposite the kirk in Palmerston Place, Edinburgh.

So it was only natural that Willie and his brother and sister should go to the Sunday school and Bible class there, and, in time, join the kirk.

Then came the war, and, like so many of us, Dr and Mrs Annan were caught up in the whirl. They left their house, so that it could be turned into a nursing home.

And Willie left, too, to die in Burma.

It was a bitter blow for Dr and Mrs Annan, yet while the ache of their loss was still in their hearts, they did a fine thing. Instead of moving back into their house when the war ended, they gave it—lock, stock and barrel—to the kirk across the road, in memory of their son.

Now the Willie Annan House is open. It has been transformed into a new hall, kirk session room, library and other meeting rooms, with a flat for the church officer. There is also a wee garden at the back which will be laid out as a rest garden for the old folk of the district.

You know, some folk say Willie Annan never came back. But surely he is there in spirit—in the house he knew, beside the kirk he loved.

FRIDAY—AUGUST 18.

A UKRAINIAN who was working in England wrote to London asking permission to withdraw his money from his local savings account. The sum involved amounted to £200, and when permission arrived from London, the money was all ready in the Post Office safe.

The Ukrainian duly presented his book, and was handed the £200. He thereupon proceeded to count the money.

At last, having satisfied himself that his £200 was all there, he handed back the money. He was merely wanting to make sure it was still safe and sound!

SATURDAY—AUGUST 19.

WORDS cannot say what that morning meant to Evelyn Dunne.

Bright and early, she set off alone down the street to catch a bus into the busy centre of Middlesbrough. From there she got another bus out to Stockton. Finally, 12 miles from home, she sat down at a typewriter to begin her very first job. Granted, it was only temporary, but, oh, it meant so much to her.

You see, Evelyn was only five when her eyesight began to give trouble. By the time she was 13 she had undergone 13 operations to try to save her sight. When no more could be done, she was trained in a school for the blind as a shorthand-typist.

So Evelyn, a small, fair-haired girl of 20, stepped out into the world of work for the first time on her own. She didn't even carry a stick. Brave lass, she started out as she means to carry on—independent.

Bravo, Evelyn! I only hope that if any of us ever have heavy odds to face up to, we will show at least a fraction of your undaunted spirit.

SUNDAY—AUGUST 20.

THEN shall the righteous shine forth as the sun in the Kingdom of their Father. Who hath ears to hear, let him hear.

MONDAY—AUGUST 21.

COME with me, back through the years to a house in Glasgow. As we stand quietly outside the window, we hear the sound of singing from a curtained room. Inside, a handful of people are gathered, listening in silent wonder to the voice of the great John McCormack.

At the piano sits Annie Tennant Carpenter, a little lady, with a smile on her face and magic in her fingers. The famous singer turns and bows to her, and begins to sing perhaps his most beautiful song of all—" I hear you calling me!"

He was singing it specially for her, and his whole heart was in it, for she had been his accompanist in the days when he was an unknown singer from Ireland. Although agent after agent wouldn't consider him, Annie Carpenter, his faithful accompanist, believed in him and stood by him. They toured together until at last his genius was recognised.

John McCormack never forgot his old friend and helper, and so it was that years later he returned to Glasgow at the height of his fame, to sing for her once again. And those who heard him that night declared he sang " I hear you calling me " as he'd never sung it before.

Today, Miss Carpenter, now in her eighties, lives in a home for elderly folk in Glasgow. Yet I know that when she plays the music John McCormack loved, she can almost hear the golden voice singing as on that evening when they met for the last time:—

" I came, do you remember, back to you . . ."

TUESDAY—AUGUST 22.

CLARK ANDERSON was only six when he fell and broke his leg. Since then he has never walked. He has also lost the use of his arms.

Today, Clark is a growing boy who must live sitting down. Every day he is lifted from bed to an armchair, from armchair to a seat at table for his meals, then back to the armchair.

Just think what that means, when laddies of Clark's age run helter-skelter at sports and trips, and go cycling and camping . . . Alas, all the fun of being young cannot be for Clark . . . He can only sit and read for a little at a time.

Although his mother has three younger children to see to as well as Clark, she gallantly went out and worked until she saved enough to buy a TV set.

What a Godsend it has been to Clark! I know it's made him so happy, his mother has sometimes been moved to tears.

When I think what TV is doing for this laddie I give thanks for its miracle . . . and for the loving mother who brought it to him.

WEDNESDAY—AUGUST 23.

LOTS of folk on holiday
On or by the sea,
Camping, tramping here or there,
Happy as can be.
Holidays? My hat, I'd say
Half the world has gone away!
Don't forget, though, lots of folk
Simply cannot roam—
Busy folk and invalids
Who must stay at home.
If a rest and change you've got
Drop a line to those who've not!

Thursday—August 24.

SILLY thought I agree . . .

But suppose each of us was born with a little gadget growing on our shoulder, and from the moment we were born it counted off the number of minutes left to us, beginning, say, with two million, and going down to one million, five hundred thousand, a hundred thousand, ten thousand, fifty, twenty, ten, five, four, three, two, one, zero!

A bit unnerving, isn't it?

But the thought occurs to me that as the minutes were counted off and the number left to us steadily decreased, you and I would use each minute to the utmost, wouldn't we?

Friday—August 25.

WILL COX has been a beadle for 11 years. He has known seven ministers in his lifetime's membership of the wee kirk at Chapelhall.

But, bless my soul, he couldn't even get a seat the other Sunday. Neither could two of the elders. The three of them had to squeeze in with the choir.

From the rows of children in front to the very back of the building, every pew was packed. So were the aisles, with folk sitting on forms that had to be brought in.

Yet a little time ago the outlook for the kirk seemed bleak, indeed. For 10 months there had been no minister, and the church seemed to be without heart.

Now the Rev. Gordon Simpson has taken over the church in his first charge. And he has worked a transformation that is almost unbelievable.

People tell you glibly the kirk is becoming less and less important in our lives today.

Don't believe it! The message of Chapelhall is that we love and need our kirk as much as ever.

SATURDAY—AUGUST 26.

NOT long ago a teenager called on his minister, and the two began talking.

" You may not be seeing much of me in future," announced the teenager. " I'm not saying I'm leaving the church, but I just don't see why I need bother to go regularly."

To the teenager's surprise, the minister nodded. " Well, well," said he, " I expect you know what you're doing, laddie. It isn't for me to plan your life. I've enough to do visiting the sick, thinking about my sermons and winding up my clocks."

" Winding up your clocks?" repeated the teenager. " I shouldn't think that's a big job."

" No, no, not a big job. But it must be done. You see, the clock in the hall gets wound every night about eleven . . . and it ticks fine. But this clock here in my study—just look at it! Pointing to five to three and the time's ten past eight! A clock that doesn't get wound up is just no good . . . and a bit of bother, eh?"

The teenager nodded thoughtfully.

" Well, well," murmured the minister, kindly, " you know your own business best, I suppose. But remember what I've been telling you about clocks. And you and I need winding up, too, regularly, so that the things of the spirit are never lost, and the power of God within is always there."

I cannot tell you what the teenager intends doing next Sunday—all I know is that to date he has not missed going to church.

SUNDAY—AUGUST 27.

WHAT I tell you in darkness, that speak ye in light: and what ye hear in the ear, that preach ye upon the housetops.

MONDAY—AUGUST 28.

AT six o'clock every Monday evening all over the country—and in many overseas lands, too—drivers of cars, vans and lorries pull into the side of the road and stop.

For a few moments they bow their heads in prayer, and their prayer is always the same. Everyone asks God's protection for all road users. They are members of the Christian Road Safety League.

It all started in 1937, when a group of motorists pledged themselves to do all in their power to make the highways and byways safer.

And wonderful to relate, from this tiny band of 16 has grown a movement that can be measured in thousands, with members all over the world.

I have seldom heard of a more worthwhile band—and I know of no brief minute of prayer that is dedicated to a better purpose.

TUESDAY—AUGUST 29.

LONG years ago I had a great-aunt who every now and then visited a lady who was reputed to come of aristocratic family.

One Sunday my great-aunt took me with her.

Eventually our hostess begged her visitor to partake of another piece of cake, and, to my astonishment, my great-aunt replied in an unusually refined voice—" Oh, no thank you, I've had an excellent sufficiency."

" Great-aunt," said I innocently, " why do you say you've had an excellent sufficiency here, and when you come to tea at our house you say you're full?"

Of course, she was furious with me. Looking back, I can sympathise with her, bless her.

Nevertheless, if people *will* put on airs and graces, they must expect a shock now and then. For it's always safest to be ourselves, wherever we may be.

WEDNESDAY—AUGUST 30.

NICE to see them walking
Arm in arm, those two—
Dad and Mum together—
As they used to do.
Thirty-three years married,
Both now going grey . . .
Nice to hear them talking
In their loving way.
Days and nights through good and ill,
Two romantic sweethearts still!

THURSDAY—AUGUST 31.

THE people of Greenock held a service that started at four o'clock in the morning and went on to ten-thirty at night.

They read the whole of the New Testament, from Matthew to Revelation.

Promptly at 4 a.m. a Salvation Army brigadier started reading aloud from St Matthew, chapter one, verse one, and from then on the reading was done in relays.

At four forty-five a man and woman on their way to work arrived and took over for a time. More early workers followed, then housewives with their shopping bags came and went, sharing the readings with various ministers.

So the marathon went on non-stop in a splendid example of Christian co-operation, until at last, at 10.30 p.m., the last word in Revelation was reached.

Altogether nearly 100 people had shared in the readings, which lasted almost 19 hours.

And why did they do it?

To show how simple it is to read the Bible, and that even during a busy working day time *can* be found to read at least a little of the word of God.

SEPTEMBER

Friday—September 1.

THERE'S an art in going to bed.

It doesn't mean merely tumbling in between the sheets and dropping off to sleep. There's more to it than that. Go to bed tonight with worries and bad feeling, and you'll wake up with a headache.

At the end of the day there ought to be at least a few minutes' quiet before bed . . . looking back over the waking hours, and trying to recall the bits of sunshine, the kindnesses, the happy things. There ought to be a conscious effort at forgiving everybody who has wounded us, and a wee prayer that God will not only take away our tiredness, but also that He will wash away any stain on our soul that we may begin a new day with a fresh, clean spirit.

Saturday—September 2.

THE other morning I watched a man stand back and admire his work in a Lanarkshire road.

Can you guess what this man had made?

A hole in the ground—deep, round and gaping.

My friend is a roadman, but for years he has been crippled with muscular dystrophy—that dread illness which wastes and withers every muscle.

As he laid his spade down to talk to me, he had to painfully prise each finger free, for they had locked on the handle. This pain is now part of his life. But it is a part that he refuses to give in to.

I left the brave roadman climbing back into the gaping hole he had created.

Soon it would be gone, the job complete. But that hole in the road will remain in my memory . . . a wonderful work of art created out of downright determination and so much pain.

SUNDAY—SEPTEMBER 3.

WHEN Jesus therefore perceived that they would come and take Him by force, to make Him a king, He departed again into a mountain Himself alone.

MONDAY—SEPTEMBER 4.

I CAME across these lines in an American church magazine—

A room of quiet, a temple of peace,
The house of faith, where doubtings cease;
A well of comfort, where hope is given,
A source of strength to make earth heaven;
A shrine for worship, a place to pray.
I found all these in my church today.

TUESDAY—SEPTEMBER 5.

I DO not think I have ever had a stranger request. It came to me in a letter from a mother, whose only daughter is today in prison.

Her mother has asked me to write or even visit her in prison, to talk to her.

The terrible thing is that this young girl—her parents' pride and joy—doesn't want to see either of them for she is too ashamed . . .

I felt I must do something . . . but what? Meanwhile, I wrote the girl a letter, but not a letter reminding her of the family she let down, for no one realises that more than the lassie herself.

Instead, I told her what's done is done, and that she must not let her mind dwell on the past. Her family love her, perhaps more than ever.

Sooner than she may think, the prison door will close behind her, and other doors will open, each leading to a new beginning and a new life.

WEDNESDAY—SEPTEMBER 6.

I HEARD somebody laugh and laugh—
It made me laugh to hear,
A hearty laugh, a jolly laugh,
The peals both loud and clear.
Now guess who laughed so loud and long
And simply couldn't stop,
A patient in a hospital
Who last week had an op!
It made me pause to think. I said—
"Maybe I need a week in bed!"

THURSDAY—SEPTEMBER 7.

TWO folk walked slowly along the street the other afternoon.

They were a grey-haired lady who leaned a little on the arm of her tall, broad and handsome son, aged twenty.

I stopped and had a chat with them, and after ten minutes there seemed so much more to say that I compelled them to turn into a cafe so that we might go on exchanging news over a cup of tea and some buttered toast.

How attentive the tall young man was to his mother. How quickly and eagerly his mother talked about his academic success and his prospects . . . and still more, of the wonderful way in which he had helped her all along, had stood by her, had given her everything he could, had been such a comfort and joy . . .

Maybe you'll understand that I was more than usually interested in all this because for eighteen years these two have been living in another town . . . and the last time I saw them was in this same street when the mother, newly widowed, and fearful of the future, was wheeling her son in a pram!

WHERE THERE'S A WILL

It's true for a swan and it's true for a man,
If you try hard enough you will find that you CAN!

DAVID HOPE

PEACE

Friendly beasts, grazing at ease,
The gentle shade of kindly trees!
Rest a moment, friend, and then
You'll stronger face the world again.

DAVID HOPE

FRIDAY—SEPTEMBER 8.

THERE was great excitement in the wee house when the painters arrived.

Indeed, I'm sure Miss Mary Anderson never dreamed she'd ever see her kitchen looking as spick and span as it was when the painters finished.

What's more, they didn't take a penny for doing the job . . . they were glad to do it. They simply turned up at Miss Anderson's door the other afternoon, carted in brushes and paper and paste, rolled up their sleeves and set to work.

The painters were her minister and one of his elders.

They knew that a shining home meant more to Miss Anderson than to most of us, for since she had to give up her job she seldom gets out of doors.

So the two men from the kirk decided that if Miss Anderson couldn't get out into the sunshine, they'd take a little sunshine to her.

I say blessed are they who roll up their sleeves to help others!

SATURDAY—SEPTEMBER 9.

BY the way, are you keeping a watch on yourself? If not, don't you think you ought to?

As the years go by—and they go so very quickly—how easy for you to deteriorate! Unpleasant thought, to be sure . . . but once you had such lofty ideals, and now? Once you were so eager to serve your church or town, but in recent years you don't feel like bothering quite so much—and, of course, bridge or golf, and so on. Once you would have blushed had you heard the sort of story you listened to the other evening without even a hint of embarrassment.

If there's dust on your jacket you flick it off.

Maybe it doesn't matter if there's dust on your soul!

SUNDAY—SEPTEMBER 10.

NO man can come to Me, except the Father which hath sent Me draw him: and I will raise him up at the last day.

MONDAY—SEPTEMBER 11.

IF you ever feel like giving up before your task is done, think of Giles Scott.

Giles was a young architect who dreamed of building a great new church. So when a cathedral was to be built at Liverpool, he began preparing plans to enter in a competition to see who would be the architect. But he was only 22 . . . he would be up against architects of twice his age and ten times his experience.

" I've given up," he told a friend. " It's no use going on. What chance have I got?"

But when his friend looked over the plans, he knew they were drawn by a master hand. Quietly, he encouraged young Giles to keep on with his work.

Believe it or not, he won the competition!

Today the cathedral stands in all its majesty on St James' Mount, Liverpool.

It will be many years before it is finished, but already the genius of Giles Scott is an inspiration to all who pass through its doors.

Not long ago, Giles Scott died. But he was no longer the struggling architect. He was Sir Giles Scott, a man who enriched our country with some of its noblest and humblest buildings—like the red telephone box.

So, as I say, if you feel like giving up—as Giles Scott once did—take heart and carry on. For what you are doing may turn out to be the finest thing you've ever done.

Tuesday—September 12.

I CONFESS that Norman Macleod meant no more to me than a name at the foot of a hymn . . .

That was before I came to hear of his moleskin kirk in Parliamentary Road, Glasgow.

A strange name, indeed, for a church—until you know that it was a place of worship that Norman in his thoughtfulness, set aside for those who might feel ashamed because they couldn't afford better than moleskin trousers or woollen shawls to go to church in.

How these humble, warm-hearted people loved this minister who worked so much and with such compassion among them . . . helping them to save a few coppers. providing the poor with free clothes, ministering to the sick and comforting those in despair.

He was a brave man whose own great strength was a clear conscience in the eyes of God.

It is no wonder that such a man was the writer of that stirring hymn, " Courage, brother, do not stumble . . . trust in God and do the right "—because that was the very trumpet call that inspired his own life.

Wednesday—September 13.

EXCEPTIONAL, exciting days—
Days no one can forget;
Such days are thrilling, wonderful,
Red-letter days, you bet!
But, odd as it may seem somehow,
The ordinary days
With routine chores and common jobs
In very humdrum ways . . .
These seem, though unspectacular,
The very nicest days there are!

THURSDAY—SEPTEMBER 14.

"DEAR Mr Gay—may I ask a favour, if you please?"

So began a letter from Australia. It was written in a rather scrawly hand with a pen inclined to blot.

I told myself it was likely a begging letter.

Bless her, the writer, nearly 90, almost blind, had only one request—and a small one at that—"I wondered, Mr Gay, if you would be kind enough to send me a sprig of heather? I used to roll in it when I was a bairn. I'd keep it here in my room . . . and maybe, at the end, somebody will see to it that it's in my hand when they lay me to rest . . ."

So, of course, the Lady of the House and I sent the heather—and we sent also a letter which we hope will warm the old soul's heart and bring back memories of those happy childhood days she enjoyed in Scotland so very long ago.

FRIDAY—SEPTEMBER 15.

ONE day Mr Shaw was giving a Scripture lesson to a class of boys at All Saints' School, Wigan. They were engrossed in the wondrous tale of how Jesus walked on the water, and there wasn't a lad listening whose thoughts weren't with the brave men who venture on dark and stormy seas.

Suddenly a hand shot up. "Please, sir!" said a voice. "Could we adopt a ship?"

Almost since that day the school has had a Young Trawlers' Group of 50 laddies. They've raised money for the Mission to Deep Sea Fishermen and they have adopted a ship. It's the fishing boat Girl Joyce.

The school has one of a pair of Bibles, inscribed with the name of the Girl Joyce, and on the boat is the other Bible, inscribed with the name of the school.

It's grand to hear of such an eager bunch of laddies.

SATURDAY—SEPTEMBER 16.

I DON'T blame Effie.

She's seven and thoughtful—a dreamy little creature with a wistful face. Her home is not in the very nicest of neighbourhoods.

The other day she was playing in a back court—playing, but also listening to half a dozen women gossiping. Presently she went indoors, and asked her mother gravely, "Mummy, when do people say *nice* things about people?"

Effie still hasn't got the answer.

SUNDAY—SEPTEMBER 17.

O PRAISE the Lord, all ye nations: praise Him, all ye people.

MONDAY—SEPTEMBER 18.

ONCE again the harvest is being gathered in.

Perhaps you are used to it, but for my own part I must confess that there is always a thrill in harvest time for me . . . the rich colours of the contented countryside, the fields golden between hedges laden with autumn fruits, the fellowship of harvesters who work hard and seem good humoured and friendly, the gathering into barns . . . it is an old, old labour that has always, for me, something new.

I am impressed every year by the mystery of the miracle of harvest . . . the buried seed, impervious to frost and snow and biting winds and drenching rain, springing up, struggling through the cold, multiplying by some inner chemistry I cannot fathom, and producing its fruit in due season. Back of the farmer's skill and the knowledge of those chemists who supply fertilisers, is surely a design and purpose beyond all human ken.

TUESDAY—SEPTEMBER 19.

THE unexpected sometimes happens.

For instance: one evening recently, Mrs Forbes was on her way home by bus. She had been to see her sister, and had found her very far from well. It was an apprehensive Mrs Forbes who travelled the few miles home, seeing nothing from the window, wondering all the time how her sister was going to cope with an invalid husband when her own strength was failing . . .

The bus was slowing down. Not that it mattered to Mrs Forbes—she had not arrived at her destination. Two people were standing. One was a middle-aged lady with a large bunch of flowers. She moved towards the door. " My son gave me these," she said to Mrs Forbes. " But I'm sure you need them more than I do."

And there, in Mrs Forbes's arms, were the glorious flowers. The stranger had descended and the bus was on its way again.

For Mrs Forbes the future is as forbidding now as ever it was . . . but those flowers and that spontaneous and unexpected kindness have given her new strength and courage.

WEDNESDAY—SEPTEMBER 20.

IT'S lots and lots of little things,
That makes a woman cry.
A weariness, a heavy wash,
A neighbour's scornful eye.
An unkind word, a word unsaid,
A faded dream . . . ah me,
What tortures to the mind and heart
Life's little things can be!
Perhaps a prayer, a smile, a song
Will help a gallant soul along!

THURSDAY—SEPTEMBER 21.

OVER the bridge and by the stream you come to a wee house with a garden in front and an orchard behind; and there, sitting on the step in the evening sunshine was a roundish woman, all smiles; and in the garden stood her " old man " seriously bethinking himself it was time to do a bit of weeding, or maybe he'd leave it till the morrow . . . and how his eyes kindled when I came in sight . . . sure *now* he had an excuse for taking things even easier than he'd been taking them . . . which was maybe why he was so hospitable, and kept me chatting there till dusk.

FRIDAY—SEPTEMBER 22.

LAST century, Sandy Grant, a Scottish settler in Canada, chose to make his home by the Shuswap Lake, British Columbia.

Not long after he had arrived, a friend showed him round the district, and Sandy was amazed at the size of everything—the trees, lakes and mountains.

All at once the friend gripped Sandy's arm and pointed out a big moose standing on a distant hill.

Of course, a moose is a type of deer—but Sandy immediately thought of the wee, sleekit, tim'rous beastie Burns wrote about! So exclaimed Sandy—

" Since ye hae mice as big as that
I wouldna like tae meet a rat—
And it maun be a guid-sized cat
Would dare to tackle sic a moose!"

The story soon got around and the settlers all laughed about it. But as the settlement grew into an important little township, they decided to call it—SICAMOUS!

There it stands to this day, a thriving community, known to the world as Sicamous—and I'm sure if old Sandy Grant was alive he'd be proud of it!

SATURDAY—SEPTEMBER 23.

AS I stood in the grey dampness of a foggy afternoon, watching an old man being laid in his last resting place, my thoughts were 30 years away.

I was thinking of a warm summer's evening spent by the banks of a placid river.

Two figures sat there with fishing rods. One was a middle-aged man with wise face and kind eyes. The other, much younger then, was Francis Gay. And we were discussing religion.

My friend told me he had thought long and hard about it, and had reached the conclusion there could be no God and no Heaven.

His arguments, it seemed to my young mind, were overwhelmingly convincing, and indeed I was strangely disturbed that such a decent, clever man should hold these opinions.

I presented my case as best I could—yet I felt hopelessly inadequate, for I could not put my beliefs and faith into the words I wanted.

In due course the two of us went our separate ways, and for many years I heard nothing of my friend. Then word came that he had died, and I slipped into the cemetery to pay my last respects.

There was a minister there, reading from the Bible. And I couldn't help thinking how pathetic it was—how infinitely saddening that the life of such a fine man should end without having been enriched by the peace and love and understanding that only a closeness with Him can give.

SUNDAY—SEPTEMBER 24.

THE law of the Lord is perfect, converting the soul: the testimony of the Lord is sure, making wise the simple.

Monday—September 25.

AT the Harvest Festival it's the custom around Stockton for Sunday school children to bring a gift of fruit or vegetables, hand it to the minister, then say a text.

Mr Charles Wasson, of Stockton, tells me that one wee girl brought a gift of a rosy apple to church for the Harvest Festival service—but she was most reluctant to part with it.

After a few moments, although she still clutched the apple, she was asked to say her text.

It was—" Hold fast to that which is good!"

Tuesday—September 26.

CAN you think of anything finer than giving up a day of the holiday to cheer a patient in a mental hospital?

Frankly, I cannot. That's why I'm proud to tell this story of Mrs Black.

Quite by chance she heard that a school friend of 50 years ago was in hospital quite near her—and longed to see her home again.

Mrs Black had not seen her friend in all these years, but she wrote to the doctor and got permission to take her friend out. So there she was with her old friend Margaret, bowling along through the lovely hills of Westmorland, sharing the glorious scenery.

What a wonderful day it was. It was 14 years since Margaret had been to Windermere, home of her childhood. They found her old home looking just as Margaret had left it, and they met her neighbours of bygone days.

We can never guess what all this meant to Margaret, but I do know that to Mrs Black this day which she gave up to an old friend of 50 years ago was, in its way, the best day of her holiday.

WEDNESDAY—SEPTEMBER 27.

HOW sad that folk should suffer pain,
That gallant hearts should break,
That grim misfortune now and then
Kind folk should overtake.
How sad . . . and yet how good to know
Some friend will understand,
And where there's need will run at once
To give a helping hand.

THURSDAY—SEPTEMBER 28.

IF ever the hand of fate seemed to be against any man, it was surely against Alex. Cowie.

During the war he had been dive-bombed, wounded, shipwrecked. He came home to Chatham to recover. But within a few hours the bombers struck again and Alex's wife and baby were killed.

Broken in heart and spirit, he set out forlornly to walk to his old home. He arrived in Aberdeen tattered, unshaven, exhausted, with his money gone and the wreckage of his life behind him.

He drifted into a little hall where good folk were providing a cup of tea for the homeless.

They called themselves the Sheret Court Mission, and the cup of tea they gave Alex. so warmed his heart that he found himself able to take up the challenge of living once more.

And since that night Alex. has never looked back. Today he has a nice home; a good job; a wife, whom he met at the mission, and a wonderful family. Indeed, he is now one of the workers at the mission which miraculously lifted him up when he was at rock-bottom.

How true it is that however black the outlook for us, there is always someone holding high a light that points the way.

Friday—September 29.

SHE was proud, mighty proud.

Her husband had built up a business too rapidly, had become a name in society, was cutting a figure till the crash came suddenly and unexpectedly. He went to prison. The beautiful home was sold. The car vanished. The splendour faded.

A friend called to see the wife when she was in a two-roomed flat, and found her with her children. It was an embarrassing moment for the woman and her visitor—who had come to offer help.

Said the wife, "You think I'm poor—how can I *ever* be poor as long as I have two children to love?"

Saturday—September 30.

THE shorter days and the longer nights are ahead . . .

Remember what Sir Harry Lauder used to say about the dark?

All his life he had a soft spot for Leerie-light-the lamp. Even as a bairn he used to watch at the window for Leerie coming along, his pole on his shoulder . . . and how thrilling it was to see the darkness behind him giving place to one halo of light after another till a long row of lights reached from end to end of the street.

It was fun, Sir Harry tells us, seeing Leerie going by—always plodding into the darkness, always leaving a trail of light behind.

As the years went by, Sir Harry realised there was more to it than that—it was a challenge to him to light a wee lamp wherever there was darkness.

And isn't that your job and mine? As we travel through this world, darkened by sorrow, what a glorious opportunity we have of lighting lamps in other people's lives, and thus when we come to the end of the road, leaving a trail of light behind us!

OCTOBER

SUNDAY—OCTOBER 1.

I WILL love Thee, O Lord, my strength.

MONDAY—OCTOBER 2.

SHORTLY before Dr Buckle died, he and his wife bravely looked into the future.

They had been companions so long, understanding and helping each other, sharing the adventure of living, comforting each other in sorrow.

But Dr Buckle was suffering from coronary thrombosis, and one evening his wife confessed—" Dearest, if I were left I should be frightened without you."

" No, no," replied her husband. " You must not think of it like that, and you must not stay indoors weeping. As soon as it is all over, you must put on your hat and pop in to see some lonely or sad folk. You'll be happy if you do!"

Dr Buckle passed on, and his widow did exactly as he had advised. How hard it was to wear a smile only she could know; but she did smile; she did pop in to see sad and lonely folk . . . and she was happy, and still is.

TUESDAY—OCTOBER 3.

OCTOBER once more! That means blustery winds and chillier weather; fewer hours of daylight; leafless trees and empty flower-beds.

Thank goodness it also means coming home to tea by a cosy fire, time to read some good books, or take up a new hobby, or long, pleasant evenings at home with friends and family.

You know, I can almost bring myself to say, " Thank goodness, it's October once more!"

Wednesday—October 4.

I DON'T think I'm the worst of all
The folk alive today.
Of virtues I have one or two—
So other people say.
I might be worse—but in that thought
Is not much joy for me,
For, oh how little am I like
The man I meant to be!

Thursday—October 5.

HE was mending a fence—an old man in the shadow of a great mountain. I looked critically at his handiwork. The wood was sound, the workmanship of the best.

" You're making a good job of it," I said.

" I have to," he replied gravely. " Can't help myself. This is my own farm. My folk have farmed this land for nigh on three hundred years. I've inherited what they left. If I were to shirk or do shoddy work I'd be letting them down !"

Friday—October 6.

IT was a dream of Francis Johnson that one day he would be a missionary. Alas, it never came true. His health wasn't up to it.

He never lost interest in mission work, and he often pictured what life must be like in these outposts. Each time he came on a new name of a mission station, he made a note of it.

And Francis is now giving a helping hand to each of these missions. He sends books and newspapers to them himself and he has given the mission addresses to many people who also send reading material.

Good for you, Francis!

SATURDAY—OCTOBER 7.

ONE day in 1778 William Cowper, the poet and hymn-writer, was so depressed that he came very near to doing away with himself. Instead of committing suicide, however, he prayed—and afterwards, with new courage, he wrote these famous lines:—

Ye fearful saints, fresh courage take—
The clouds ye so much dread
Are big with mercy, and will break
In blessings on your head.

SUNDAY—OCTOBER 8.

O LORD, rebuke me not in Thine anger, neither chasten me in Thy hot displeasure.

MONDAY—OCTOBER 9.

I DON'T suppose anyone will ever know how many bunches of flowers Mrs Cannon gave away.

She gave them away by the dozen . . . to old people, to folk who were kept in bed or indoors by illness, and to the church where she worshipped.

Now, what's so special about all this, you may ask? Well, it happens that although Mrs Cannon loves flowers and gave so many away she didn't even have a garden ! Indeed, she lived up three flights of stairs in a single room.

But, bless her, she didn't spend the little she was able to save on wee extras for herself. Instead, she regularly went into a florist's, bought a lovely bunch of flowers and took them to some home where the sun wasn't shining very brightly.

Why she did it, no one knows. Her husband, who passed on many years ago, was a gardener, and this may have been her way of keeping his memory fresh.

TUESDAY—OCTOBER 10.

FIFTY members of Carrick Knowe Church Youth Club, Edinburgh, descended with spades and forks and barrows on an unused piece of ground in the surrounds of the kirk.

They dug and raked and hoed—and soon they had transformed what had once been rather an eyesore into a lovely brown patch of clean earth. Next they planted row upon row of—potatoes!

Then in the autumn the band marched on their plot again, this time armed with forks. One by one the shaws were lifted and a bountiful harvest of new potatoes was gathered in.

But the young folk weren't finished yet—not by a long chalk.

They piled the potatoes into a barrow and set out on a trek round the houses in the parish. And whenever they came to the door of an old soul they knew hadn't much to come and go on, they stopped, scooped a bucketful of potatoes from their barrow and handed it over.

I'm told they visited so many homes they lost count of the number of bucketsful they distributed.

Well done, Carrick Knowe! It's one of the nicest harvest thanksgivings I've ever heard of.

WEDNESDAY—OCTOBER 11.

NOW autumn brings her sunset hues
To every falling leaf,
And woods and gardens all ablaze,
Are rich beyond belief.

Perhaps we feel a little sad
From long bright days to part—
Yet let us keep, though winter comes,
A springtime in our heart.

THURSDAY—OCTOBER 12.

LORD TENNYSON'S son told this story:

My father said that when he was stopping at a coffee-house in London, Carlyle had come to smoke a pipe with him in the evening, and the talk turned on the immortality of the soul; upon which Carlyle said: "Eh, old Jewish rags! You must clear your mind of all that. Why should we expect a hereafter? Your traveller comes to an inn, and he takes his bed; it's only for one night, he leaves next day, and another man takes his place and sleeps in the bed he has vacated."

My father answered: "Your traveller comes to his inn and lies down in his bed, and leaves the inn in the morning, and goes on his way rejoicing with the sure and certain hope and belief that he is going somewhere where he will sleep the next night."

Then Edward Fitzgerald, who was present, said: "You have him there."

FRIDAY—OCTOBER 13.

PUKI is a bright-eyed little dog not unlike a Corgi.

And, bless my soul, how he works for others.

Toss down a penny, and Puki picks it up so fast it's in his mouth before you can see how it's done. Toss down another and Puki drops the first on the floor beside it—then picks up both! Toss pennies all round the room, and Puki's after them, picking them all up like a vacuum cleaner!

Once he managed thirteen pennies in his mouth at one time—and he's equally good with half-crowns!

Puki's owners are hotelkeepers and the money he collects is sent to various charities.

Many's the honourable mention I've made of those who help others, so I'm dashed if I'm going to pass by little Puki without a "well done" pat on the back!

NEVER TOO OLD !

Crossing little bridges,
Paddling in the stream,
Consigning to the current
Every busy scheme—
When such joys no pleasure hold
Then I will be VERY old !

DAVID HOPE

CONTRASTS

If life were always roses,
It would indeed be joy,
Yet would it? This I ponder :
For swiftly pleasures cloy.
We need December chills to show
How sweet in June the rose can blow.

DAVID HOPE

SATURDAY—OCTOBER 14.

I KNOW that little Ian couldn't tell just what happened on that day three years ago.

He just ran out of the school gates, caught a fleeting glimpse of a corporation bus bearing down on him—and that's all . . .

When he woke up in hospital he felt a funny pain in his leg—and then through the mists of consciousness he realised his leg wasn't there any more.

When the day came for him to try his new artificial leg how disappointed he was. For it was sore and uncomfortable, and he just couldn't make it work.

The young doctor in the ward tried everything to encourage Ian. Finally, he took him aside. "Of course, you'll be able to walk," he said, "and run and play football, too. If you just keep trying."

Then he paused and added quietly, "I know . . . look." With that, he pulled up his own trouser leg—and showed Ian that he, too, had an artificial leg.

I don't know of anything that could have helped Ian more. For, from that day, he grew better and better in the use of his artificial leg.

SUNDAY—OCTOBER 15.

FOR we are labourers together with God: ye are God's husbandry, ye are God's building.

MONDAY—OCTOBER 16.

A LITTLE boy surprised his mother by saying that when he grew up he wanted to be a minister—not a bus driver or space-rocket pilot.

"Why a minister?" asked Mother.

"Well," said the laddie, "if some of us don't make up our minds to be ministers, there won't be anyone to bury us when we die!"

TUESDAY—OCTOBER 17.

YOU would easily know Martha Robby and May Hamilton.

They walk together, shop together and go to church together. In fact, they're always together and, if you look for the two happiest faces together in the street, that's sure to be them.

Martha and May live in a little house which they manage together. They enjoy the radio together and, when it's not on, they sit together, a picture of content, one reading aloud as the other listens and knits.

A remarkable couple, indeed. But that isn't the whole story.

Martha and May have been firm friends for 45 years now. Yet the amazing thing is they have never seen one another. Martha can just distinguish light from dark. May has been blind almost since birth. So they even share darkness together.

Indeed, it was their blindness that brought them into this friendship all these years ago at a school for the blind.

That fine school helped to give them confidence in themselves and to earn their own living. But most of all, it gave Martha and May one another—and what a blessed thing that has been.

WEDNESDAY—OCTOBER 18.

THE children playing in the court—
Those lively girls and boys,
What boundless energy they have,
And, oh, the noise, the noise!
Though growing old, on them I love
To keep a watchful eye:
And, spite of tears, I lose my years,
And, oh, how young am I!

THURSDAY—OCTOBER 19.

I SAT back in a chair, closed my eyes, and listened to a book talking!

Every day Robert Gladwell goes to a studio in London, switches on a microphone, and sits with an open book. For over an hour he reads and reads.

By the time he is finished another three long-playing records have been made for the talking-book library.

Already the library contains two million records—140,000 different books all read in the same way. What a magnificent service—and all free to the five and a half thousand who love books, but are blind.

Of course, no one man could do all the reading. So every day four readers add more and more pages to the books, from Dickens to detective stories.

These story-tellers give of their time ungrudgingly and still the demand grows. Indeed, it must be a task that will never end; yet I am sure it will never want for willing helpers.

FRIDAY—OCTOBER 20.

IN my great stupid way I was talking to a little maid the other evening, and I said, "And what will you do when you grow up?"

She looked at me with grave eyes, and said, "Mr Gay, must I grow up?"

Who would know how to answer that? Not I.

But the words of William Butler Yeats came flooding back into my mind. . . .

The land of fairy,
Where nobody gets old and godly and grave,
Where nobody gets old and crafty and wise,
Where nobody gets old and bitter of tongue.

That, says Yeats, is the Land of Heart's Desire. A few folk find it . . . the years pass but they don't get old!

SATURDAY—OCTOBER 21.

GREATLY daring, may I venture to advise you now and again to take a hint from that wise man, George Horace Lorimer :—

It's good to have money, and the things that money can buy ; but it's good also to check up once in a while and make quite sure that you haven't lost the things that money can't buy."

SUNDAY—OCTOBER 22.

WHEN thou liest down, thou shalt not be afraid: yea, thou shalt lie down, and thy sleep shall be sweet.

MONDAY—OCTOBER 23.

ANN is only four—a lively, pretty wee girl with long dark hair and rosy cheeks.

Every morning her mother takes Ann over to her granny's. Ann has lots of wee pals there, but she has a big job, too, for her grandmother is both deaf and dumb—and Ann is her ears and mouth.

All Gran's orders are passed to the butcher, baker and grocer through Ann's lips. She answers the door and chatters away in the deaf and dumb language all day long.

Yet Ann has never had a lesson in the language in her life. When she was only two she seemed to realise how much her gran depended on her, and she began to pick up the sign language. Ever since she was three she's been her granny's constant companion, making her silent world a little easier to bear.

But soon it will be time for Ann to go to school—and a sad day that will be for Gran. For not only will she lose her link with the outside world, she'll lose the most faithful wee friend a granny ever had.

TUESDAY—OCTOBER 24.

IF ever you read your Bible, spare a thought for William Tyndale, martyred in the Low Countries in 1536. Your Bible owes a good deal to him—for he was a pioneer among the translators into English.

Strange that this man who over 400 years ago enriched men so much should, at the end, be so poor that when in prison he wrote to the local authorities: "If it please you, be so good as to send me a warmer cap, a candle and a piece of cloth to patch my leggings."

Remember William Tyndale.

WEDNESDAY—OCTOBER 25.

IF you've made a mess of things—
Much that you regret,
If your heart is grieved because
You just can't forget;
Don't, for ever looking back,
Yesterday deplore . . .
With a bit of faith and pluck
You can start once more!

THURSDAY—OCTOBER 26.

DON'T throw mud—it makes your hands filthy. Maybe it's unnecessary to go on to say that you shouldn't talk scandal or say unkind things about others, or make up tales . . . doing so can hurt neighbours and friends. It can break hearts. It can do untold damage.

But there's another reason why you shouldn't say unkind things about folk . . . doing so hurts you! It spoils you.

So, even though it means repeating myself more than once, I say: don't throw mud!

FRIDAY—OCTOBER 27.

WHAT a wealthy man old Diogenes must have been! He lived about 400 years before Christ . . . and was so poor, they say, that his house was a tub. Nothing more. No rates or taxes for that. He did no work—and had no weekly insurance to pay. But he managed to live—and to enjoy living.

One day the greatest man alive paid the old Greek a visit. He was Alexander, and he said to Diogenes: "Is there anything I can do for you?"

"Yes," replied the poor rich man, "move a step to one side, please, so that I can see the sun!"

SATURDAY—OCTOBER 28.

JOHN was a newsvendor, who every night for years stood outside a cinema, selling papers.

People got to know him, but none perhaps so well as the police. They all knew John's friendly nod and his loyalty to the job when often he and they were the only souls about in a cold, wet street.

So when John fell ill and was whisked into hospital, his friends the Bobbies wanted to send him fruit and sweets and cigarettes. But alas for their good intentions . . . he'd been put on a special diet and such things were forbidden him.

Then they heard that John dearly loved flowers . . . and that's why an officer ordered fresh flowers for John the newsvendor every other day.

How sad I am to tell you that John died. But I know that to the end the flowers the police sent him meant more to him than they'll ever know.

SUNDAY—OCTOBER 29.

AND now abideth faith, hope, charity, these three; but the greatest of these is charity.

MONDAY—OCTOBER 30.

I DOUBT if you could have found a happier couple than Magnus Simpson and his wife Nellie.

A friend of mine popped in to see Magnus and Nellie and after a while they began to sing. That day it was their favourite song—" I'll walk beside you "—and, somehow, it seemed so fitting for they had, indeed, always walked together through life, sharing their joys and sorrows.

A few days later Nellie fell ill . . . and was taken to hospital. Magnus was with her when she died.

For a week or so Magnus himself lingered on, heartbroken, not knowing where to turn. Then alas, he, too, had to be taken to hospital. I am told that just before he died a smile lit up his face, as if his heart had been healed because he knew he was going to meet his beloved Nellie.

Magnus was laid to rest beside her. Yet in the hearts of the mourners there could be no sadness, for they knew that the promise the old couple had so often made to each other had been fulfilled :—

" *I'll look into your eyes and hold your hand,*
I'll walk beside you to the promised land . . ."

TUESDAY—OCTOBER 31.

A CONSUMPTIVE young man arrived at a U.S.A. sanatorium with a note from his home doctor. The note said :—

" My prescription for this patient is fresh air, fresh eggs, and Robert Louis Stevenson."

Said the resident doctor in the institution :—" Great ! See that the treatment is followed."

To some of you who are tired and anxious I recommend the courage, good humour and gallant spirit of R. L. S. It's astonishing to what achievements they can inspire a poor, weak body.

NOVEMBER

Wednesday—November 1.

AND now for fog or storm or snow—
And sunshine on and off ;
You're pretty sure to wheeze or ache
Or sniff or sneeze or cough.
Though winter chills bring vexing ills
Don't moan too often, please ;
And I suggest you do your best
To smile between each sneeze !

Thursday—November 2.

MR MAC has passed on.

I cannot tell you what his creed was. Most likely he was a staunch Presbyterian. But he may have been a Baptist or Congregationalist or Roman Catholic for anything I know.

What I do know is that people in his neighbourhood turned at once to him for help or sympathy. That even the dogs loved him, and waited for him to pat them. That for years he sent me a pound now and then, asking me to pass it on to help somebody.

Even now I know very little about him—but two folk to whom he was a friend in good times and ill have written to tell me that Mr Mac spent his whole life going out of his way to comfort or bless others.

As I say, he has passed on—and surely his kindly spirit is at rest, for I hardly think that when he passed over, St Paul would ask if he were a Presbyterian or a Baptist or what.

I have a feeling that St Paul would shake his hand and say—" Nice to see you, Mac. Heard a lot about you. Walk right in and make yourself at home. There's been a front seat in Heaven reserved for you for a long time !"

FRIDAY—NOVEMBER 3.

I CANNOT blame people for being depressed—I am often depressed myself. But if—as sometimes happens—people I meet are, as you might say, " wallowing " in depression and making themselves and everybody else miserable by gathering up armfuls of everything that's wrong in this old world, I lose my patience, turn on my heel, and remark, as Jay Franklin once did: " The times are not so bad as they seem . . . they couldn't be!"

SATURDAY—NOVEMBER 4.

IMAGINE a holiday hotel where every guest takes his own chair!

It's true, I assure you, and the chair goes with him into every meal and even to his room at night.

They are, of course, wheel-chairs, and the people who use them can't get about without them because they're all stricken with polio.

But these gallant folk don't let a thing like that spoil their holiday when they get to the Northern Lantern Hotel, Lytham St Annes.

The hotel has been specially laid out just for them . . . for one thing, there isn't even a single step, far less a stair, between any of the four floors!

All the going up and down is by ramp, or a lift that the holidaymakers work themselves. And what a thrill it is for them, all sorely handicapped as they are, to be able to go " upstairs " without the need of a helping hand.

SUNDAY—NOVEMBER 5.

FOR wisdom is better than rubies; and all the things that may be desired are not to be compared to it.

MONDAY—NOVEMBER 6.

CHARLES HADDON SPURGEON, one of the greatest preachers of all time, could say a lot in a few words. Thus:

Of two evils choose neither.

It needs more skill than I can tell
To play the second fiddle well.

Feel for others . . . in your pocket.

All sunshine, and nothing else, makes a desert.

A lie travels round the world while truth is putting on her boots.

TUESDAY—NOVEMBER 7.

HEARD of the little girl who began crying when she was just about ready to go to school one morning during her first term? There she was, all ready for off, and suddenly the tears came.

"Really," exclaimed Mum a little impatiently, "you can't go on like this! You're a big girl now. Why in the world have you to cry just because you don't want to go to school?"

The child took a deep breath before explaining: "I'm not crying because I don't want to go to school," said she. "I'm crying because I want to stay at home."

WEDNESDAY—NOVEMBER 8.

THE world is pretty big, Lord,
And lots of folk are bad.
To see their sin and folly
Must make You very sad.
Lord, make bad people better;
Let good folk braver be;
And when You cleanse the many,
Begin, O Lord, with me!

THURSDAY—NOVEMBER 9.

IF you were to go any Sunday to Miss Findlay's church, and if you watched her from the corner of your eye, you might notice that during the sermon she hardly ever has her eyes on the minister.

Believe it or not, Miss Findlay writes out the whole service—both morning and evening. She notes down the hymns, lessons, prayers, even the sermon—all in longhand. And when she gets back to her home she copies everything out again so that by the time she's finished it's almost word for word what the minister said.

Then comes the loveliest part of the whole thing. Miss Findlay knows a number of elderly people who can't get to church any more—so she passes round the carefully-written service so that they can, in a way, share in the worship, think about the sermon and maybe sing the hymns quietly, even though they weren't able to be at church themselves.

It just shows there's no end of ways in which we all can be of service to others.

FRIDAY—NOVEMBER 10.

YOU'LL come through, friend.

Most likely you feel sure at this moment that you will not. There is sickness in the house, and you are worried so much that you are in a panic. Or money troubles are crowding upon you, and you just don't know which way to turn or what to do for the best. Or a friend or relative has died, and you are so stricken with grief and these dark days seem so unbearably lonely that you are sure you cannot endure much longer . . .

Friend, what I have to say to you sounds commonplace, but it is eternally true: with patience and courage and faith you'll come through.

SATURDAY—NOVEMBER 11.

WITH Armistice Day in our thoughts, it may be worth our while to consider the words of one of the greatest preachers of modern times—Dr Fosdick. He tells us :

Sometimes I turn my back on the mad world where men trust to force, and come into this church alone, and look up at the cross above the altar.

As I do so, a voice seems to say—" I am the symbol of apparent failure. I represent the crucifixion of love by men of violence. They succeeded that day on Calvary. I was defeated. Yet long ago they passed away, as did the empires founded on violence . . . but I am still here, waiting.

" There is no way out of human misery but by love. Whoever believes in force trusts in a god who cannot create or organise anything permanent. In the long run, it is only love that does not fail."

SUNDAY—NOVEMBER 12.

FOR God so loved the world, that He gave His only begotten Son, that whosoever believeth in Him should not perish, but have everlasting life.

MONDAY—NOVEMBER 13.

HERE'S a recipe which—I hope—will be taken in the right spirit.

It comes from America, and is said to have been written by a schoolgirl in Georgia:

Take a natural-born fool, add two or three drinks of liquor, and mix the two in a high-powered car. After the fool is thoroughly soaked, place foot on the gas and release the brakes. In due time remove from wreckage, place in a black satin-lined box, and garnish with flowers.

TUESDAY—NOVEMBER 14.

MRS MACINTYRE was brought up in the days of lamplight and gas. Yet in six years she used more than a mile of fuse wire.

It all began when a friend showed her how to bend fuse wire into little frames. Then, by stretching nylon over the frames she learned to make—you'll never guess—lovely flowers.

The hobby fascinated her so much that she taught it to her daughter. The two of them have made hundreds of sweet peas, orchids, roses, primroses, daffies, all beautifully dyed in colours with stems and leaves—and all from old nylon stockings!

What's more, their flowers have gone all over the world and the money they bring in is used to help care for animals at a refuge near Carlisle.

WEDNESDAY—NOVEMBER 15.

NO use pretending everything
Is right as right can be—
One glance around, it won't be long
Before you find a lot that's wrong.
But take another look, my friend—
You'll see for your delight,
The good, the lovely, is not rare—
There's something worthwhile everywhere!

THURSDAY—NOVEMBER 16.

I RECENTLY came across this quotation from Dale Carnegie's writings which I think is well worth passing on:

"You can make more friends in two months by becoming interested in other people than you can in two years by trying to get other people interested in you."

FRIDAY—NOVEMBER 17.

HOW many of us fully appreciate what we owe to firemen?

Did you know for instance, that they save thousands of lives every year? Think what that means in cold facts—thousands of folk like you, or me, are alive today because of the men who can never really sit back without knowing they may be called upon to meet danger at any hour of the day or night.

There is little glamour in the day of a fireman, although it may look exciting as the shining red engine races past, bell clanging and brass gleaming. But it's a different story when the fingers are frozen by the icy water that pours from the hoses they struggle to hold on to, when the eyes are red raw with smoke and the lungs are seared . . . and there's a danger of buildings crashing down at any moment.

Thank God for men like these.

SATURDAY—NOVEMBER 18.

I MET him in a busy street on a dark, raw day, and I said, " It's a bitter wind, and no mistake."

My old friend nodded, and replied with a whimsical smile, " You're right, Francis. But until we met I was thinking of my garden, and seeing it in my mind's eye —the sweet-peas like rainbows and the lawn newly cut. My trouble, old chap, was that the wind had dropped and the sun was so hot that really I had to close my eyes as I sat in a deck chair under . . . ."

But I was away up the street.

SUNDAY—NOVEMBER 19.

HE that hath pity upon the poor lendeth unto the Lord; and that which he hath given will He pay him again.

MONDAY—NOVEMBER 20.

THERE'S a lot of shovelling in a ton of coal . . .

But it didn't bother Mrs Bell. When the load was dumped in the back lane, the dust had hardly settled before she was out with her household shovel.

She could only take a little coal at a time, but bit by bit she shovelled the whole 20 hundredweight into . . . her neighbour's cellar. Oh no, it wasn't Mrs Bell's coal—it was for an old man next door.

But that's not the only point about this story. Believe it or not, Mrs Bell had to do all her shovelling with only one hand, for she lost her right arm some years ago. It happened quite simply, too. She pricked a finger on a pin left in some curtains she was washing. She was poisoned so badly the arm had to be removed to save her life.

So if ever you're feeling down in the dumps, think of Mrs Bell. She'll lift you up—with one hand!

TUESDAY—NOVEMBER 21.

I LIKE the story of the grocer in Beverly Hills, California. If you called at his shop any Sunday morning you'd find the door locked . . . and a little card saying pointedly: " Gone to Church—where you ought to be!"

WEDNESDAY—NOVEMBER 22.

SURE that things for you will be
Worse tomorrow than today?
Certain that your luck is out,
Try as bravely as you may?
Don't get too disheartened, friend,
At the way life seems to go.
Good luck may be yours quite soon . . .
Guess you just don't know, you know!

THURSDAY—NOVEMBER 23.

NEARLY 40 years ago two London men, who felt life was good to them, decided to try to do something for others less fortunate.

From that little meeting there grew up a band of men who, by simply saving every Victorian penny they came across, have worked mighty works.

Believe it or not, they endowed no fewer than 16 children's cots in hospitals before the Health Service came along. Since then they've given away £1000 a year.

Not one penny goes into the bank, either! If they did, that would be the end of them, for they're so old they wouldn't be allowed out again.

No, the Victorian pennies are converted into silver and notes, then circulated again and again as change —and so they keep turning up . . . to be collected . . . then circulated again . . .

So I say hurrah for the merry penny men!

FRIDAY—NOVEMBER 24.

ALL that happened the other day was that I decided to turn aside as I went to the office. I just turned up a side street and went up the stairs. At the door I paused. Somebody was singing.

I walked in. I found Mrs Forbes washing up at the sink . . . and a big washing-up, too, for there are eight of them, all told, in the family. And, great daft chap that I am, I said : " Hello ! Good-morning, Mrs Forbes. Obviously you enjoy washing up !"

And she turned, stood with her arms akimbo, and looked me up and down, she did (I told the Lady of the House about it afterwards) and she said : " Well, of all things Mr Gay ! Enjoy it? I hate the very sight and sound and smell of it . . . that's why I sing !"

After all, you hardly expect a mere man . . .

A SEASIDE VILLAGE

A village I know beside the sea,
Where the waves and the driving spray blow free.
And inland, whenever I'm forced to dwell
I miss the song of the restless swell,
And the lighthouse tower and cheerful light
Flashing along the shore at night.

DAVID HOPE

CHRISTMAS EVE

We sing again the songs so dear,
The tale of love that casts out fear;
Oh grant that Christmas grace be found
Within my heart the whole year round!

DAVID HOPE

SATURDAY—NOVEMBER 25.

I LIKE the wee tale of the loving wife who rang up the doctor one morning recently and said, "Oh is that you, Doctor? It's about my husband. He was to have come to see you this morning, but he really doesn't feel well enough. He says he'll be along as soon as he's a bit better."

And of course there is the story of the patient who suffered from insomnia. "I just can't sleep, Doctor," he said over and over again. "And it's getting me down. There are times when I feel like killing myself. What shall I do?"

"Do nothing," snapped the medical man. "Leave it to me!"

SUNDAY—NOVEMBER 26.

IF ye abide in Me and My words abide in you, ye shall ask what ye will, and it shall be done unto you.

MONDAY—NOVEMBER 27.

ONCE upon a time—so I am informed, though quite frankly I don't believe a word of it—a missionary was walking briskly along a jungle path when a lion appeared. As the missionary was unarmed, he felt sure his last moment had come. Anyhow, down he went on his knees, put his hands together, and prayed.

To his astonishment (as he observed with one eye) the lion also went down on its knees and bowed its head.

"Ah," exclaimed the missionary, feeling more hopeful, "I see you also believe in prayer."

"No," replied the lion, "I am not saying my prayers. I am saying grace before meat."

TUESDAY—NOVEMBER 28.

FROM the Sanskrit of Kali-Das comes this wise saying: " Today well lived makes every yesterday a dream of happiness, and every morrow a vision of hope."

WEDNESDAY—NOVEMBER 29.

GOOD resolutions, Mr Gay
Made solemnly on New Year's Day—
The kindly things he'd do and say,
Though none beside him knew them.
Gosh, how the days and moments run . . .
The year seems scarcely yet begun !
If Francis means to get things done,
Then he must up and do them !

THURSDAY—NOVEMBER 30.

THERE'S nothing quite like a cheery fire on a cold November night, is there?

It sets me thinking of the Tullochs in the Shetlands.

Old Andrew Tulloch and his wife live in a low, turf-roofed croft-house. Perhaps the most remarkable thing about the house is the great open fireplace that takes up the whole of one wall.

It has given them warmth and comfort during many winters. It has been Mrs Tulloch's stove.

Indeed, the fire has been out only five times in the last 70 years ! Even now, old Andrew's last job at night is to build up fresh peats on the embers so that the fire will greet them again next morning.

That's why, as I look into the dancing flames of my own fire, I think of Andrew Tulloch and the light that has glowed almost unceasing from the single window of his house. I feel that the sight of the home-fire burning is surely one of the greatest blessings we have.

DECEMBER

FRIDAY—DECEMBER 1.

I LIKE the story of the unwashed heckler in Hyde Park who found himself in deep waters. A minister with courage enough to face a rather amused and not very helpful audience was preaching with all his heart when the heckler shouted, " We've had Christianity in the world for nearly two thousand years—and what difference has it made?"

Like a flash the open-air preacher replied : " There's been water on this planet for millions of years—and what difference has it made to you?"

The laugh was not against the minister but against the unwashed heckler, as it deserved to be.

And of course, what difference does Christianity make to anybody if they stand aloof from it?

SATURDAY—DECEMBER 2.

HENRY PURCELL was little more than a boy when he was apprenticed to the Abbey organist at Westminster, yet the master had to admit that his pupil was even more gifted than he himself. So he did a noble thing. He stood down in favour of his pupil and made Purcell organist of Westminster Abbey.

Glorious music flowed from his fingers and, one day, they struck a stirring trumpet tune. It soared to every corner of the Abbey and thrilled even the composer himself. Hastily he wrote it down and scribbled at the top of the sheet, " The Trumpet Tune." He'd think of a fitting title when he had a moment to do so.

Alas, he never had. He was only 37 when he died, and was buried under the organ he loved so much.

A sad story, perhaps. Yet for 300 years Purcell's trumpet tune has lived to honour him.

SUNDAY—DECEMBER 3.

BUT the word of God grew and multiplied.

MONDAY—DECEMBER 4.

MAISIE began work in a cafe recently—and a very attractive waitress she makes. Two things happened during her first week, and both surprised her.

One was the loss of her feet at the end of the first day. At least, she thought she'd lost them for ever! Arrived back home, she dragged her shoes off two swollen feet and wept . . . she was sure she was crippled for life. Anyhow, she carried trays for miles next day, and by the end of the week her feet were behaving remarkably well.

The second surprise was a happy one. Maisie had Thursday afternoon off. She was back on the job on Friday morning—and the first person she spoke to was a waitress who handed her three shillings and sixpence. " What's this for?" asked Maisie.

" Oh," was the reply, " that's your share of yesterday afternoon's tips . . . we all share and share alike, you know!"

That made Maisie think . . . and when she told me about it, it made me think, too.

TUESDAY—DECEMBER 5.

THOUGH life can for some seem utterly hopeless the most astonishing things can happen. It may be that if only you try again, that if you hang on a bit longer, what seems impossible might occur—some altogether new and unexpected turn of events which would alter everything for you.

I beg of you to keep on a bit longer.

Don't end it all . . . start fresh.

WEDNESDAY—DECEMBER 6.

GOD bless sick folk who find each day
Both wearisome and long ;
God give them patience, courage, hope—
And in their hearts a song.

And God bless all who care for such,
And try to ease the pain—
And ask for nothing but to see
Their loved ones well again !

THURSDAY—DECEMBER 7.

SEEK and ye shall find.

Familiar words. You don't need me to tell you they come from the New Testament, and that Jesus said them.

What a glorious promise they contain . . . seek God, and you will find Him ; search for the good and lovely things in this world, and you will discover them at every turn. Let us be glad indeed that if we seek, we find.

One minute, though. What would you say if I suggested that these five words are actually among the most terrible and frightening that Christ ever uttered?

For He said that if you seek you will find . . . and if you are looking for the worst you may be sure to come across it wherever you go. Search for the ugly and unlovely and unhealthy things, and you'll gather a harvest which will make you miserable indeed. Look out for the worst in the men and women you meet—you'll come across so much that is shattering that maybe you'll commit suicide because you are a disillusioned cynic with nothing in your heart but despair.

Seek, and ye shall find . . . make sure you're looking for the best.

FRIDAY—DECEMBER 8.

O LORD, help me not to fuss today.

It's a little prayer really. Suppose between getting out of bed and breakfast you say these words to yourself—what happens? Why, they do something (even though it isn't much) to steady you down, to calm you when you are tempted to go off the handle, to remind you not to make mountains of molehills, to warn you against rushing around, getting het-up, and so on.

If it is true, as somebody has said, that we make half our troubles ourselves, surely the folk who try not to fuss and who rarely get in a flap are most likely to make the best use of each day as it comes.

SATURDAY—DECEMBER 9.

"YEARS ago," Mr Anderson tells me, "I didn't think much of it. I know better now."

He was referring to a recipe his mother gave him when he was a teenager. It was not a recipe for soups or stews or cakes or pies. It was a recipe for happiness . . . and, quite frankly, it sounded so simple that, well, it just wasn't worth remembering.

The recipe was this: A bright fire, a kettle simmering on the hob, a box of sugar plums on the chimneypiece, and time and inclination to think about the nice things people tell you.

That's all there was to it.

Rather footling? There'll be lots of young folk who, reading this, will be scornful.

But Mr Anderson has lived a number of years, has learnt a good deal, and has come to the conclusion that the recipe for happiness his mother gave him years ago isn't to be made fun of and lightly disregarded . . . for surely anybody who does as she advised will gather a lot of happiness every day.

SUNDAY—DECEMBER 10.

HONOUR thy father and thy mother: that thy days may be long upon the land which the Lord thy God giveth thee.

MONDAY—DECEMBER 11.

COME to think of it, some of the finest and most useful lives I've seen lived have been lived by very ordinary people.

I'm thinking of a shepherd of the hills who tends his sheep and never loses one . . . and has always time to talk of the things of the spirit if ever a tourist happens to meet him.

I'm thinking of a widow who goes to the office every day, and is never absent from her Sunday school class, where she is faithful and patient and loving.

I'm thinking of a little man who works at the gasworks, earns his money, gives good service, and has gathered round him a few folk interested in birds. They go bird-watching whenever they can.

Nothing spectacular about any of these people. You can depend on it they'll never receive high awards—medals or titles. But they don't need them. They are among the very happiest folk living. They're getting just about as much out of any week as anybody ever can, and for them each day is satisfying.

TUESDAY—DECEMBER 12.

A FRIEND tells me that in his travels recently he passed a church outside which was a large notice asking: WHAT IS MISSING FROM THIS CH CH?

Being very slow in the uptake I had to consider a minute before the penny dropped.

WEDNESDAY—DECEMBER 13.

SAY a kindly word today,
Help a friend along,
Give a bit of praise somewhere,
Sing a merry song.
Brighten life for someone else
As you go your way . . .
Funny thing, but you will find
You've a happy day!

THURSDAY—DECEMBER 14.

I RECEIVED a letter from Canada with 20 dollars —and a strange request.

The writer is now an old woman who emigrated to Canada many years ago. It seems that because of her circumstances then, she left the country without paying two bills—one a tax of £2, and the other a dentist's account for thirty shillings.

You might think that the passage of years would have dimmed the memory of two small debts. Instead, time did the opposite. Often she lay awake at night, worrying about the money she owed. She often meant to do something about it, but there was no one left in Scotland in whom she felt she could confide. Finally, she wrote to me.

Now here is the wonderful thing about her request. She wants to repay her debts twofold!

So I've paid the tax office double what was owed them—but I'm happy to say I have not paid the dentist! When I explained things to him, he said the old woman had paid over and over again in the anguish and remorse she suffered, and he asked me to use the money to help others in need!

Now there's no saying the good the money will do—all because an old woman could not rest until she had paid what was due—with interest.

FRIDAY—DECEMBER 15.

ONCE upon a time there were three boys—Joe, Bob and Ian.

I'm afraid they were not-too-good boys. In fact, they landed in Paisley's Kibble Reform School.

When they finished their time there, they went out into the world. Joe took up farming, Bob and Ian went into the services. All three made good.

Now, you might think they had seen enough of the reform school, mightn't you? But not a bit of it.

Joe, Bob and Ian knew their success in life was largely due to the help and guidance they'd received at the reform school. So they resolved to return, whenever possible, every Christmastide to share in the festivities. They felt they were " coming home."

What a shining example these three must be to the boys sitting around them. And what a nice way of saying " Thanks."

SATURDAY—DECEMBER 16.

I LIKE the answer of the small boy who was asked by his Sunday school teacher—" What is loving kindness?"

Said he—" Well, miss, if Mum gave me a slice of bread and butter that would be kindness. If she put jam on, that would be loving kindness."

I don't know what answer the Sunday school teacher expected. I am not sure what theologians would say was a good description of loving kindness. But I do know this—That love loves to give.

SUNDAY—DECEMBER 17.

FOR to this end Christ both died, and rose, and revived, that He might be Lord both of the dead and living.

MONDAY—DECEMBER 18.

RECENTLY a woman found herself in a rather awkward situation. She and her very small daughter had taken a taxi from King's Cross, London, and the driver was a coloured man.

"Mummy," inquired the little girl in a very shrill voice, "why is the driver so black?"

Her mother knew intuitively that the driver was embarrassed, so she tried to think of something that wouldn't hurt his feelings.

"Well, darling," she replied, "it's this way. God makes people much as he makes flowers. You know we have differently coloured flowers in our gardens—and in the same way people may be white or brown or black or yellow or red. Don't you think that makes things a lot more interesting?"

"Yes," agreed the child.

The driver was smiling. "Ma'am," said he, "when my lil' girl grows up a bit, and asks me why some people are white, I'll be happy to know what to tell her."

TUESDAY—DECEMBER 19.

"OH," exclaimed the Lady of the House, "I love winter!" There she was curled up in the big chair before a roaring fire, her slippers on the rug, her arms round a library book.

"You look the picture of idleness," I told her.

"It's glorious to have nothing to do just now and then," said she. "And the best of all," she went on musingly, "is that it's quite a long time to spring!"

"Come, come," I began. "Springtime brings the daffodils and singing birds and longer days . . ."

"And spring cleaning!" said she with a shudder.

Then she sighed happily, opened her book, and lost herself in a romance.

WEDNESDAY—DECEMBER 20.

IF in this land when Christmas dawns—
A little child should weep
Because no Santa came to him
While he was fast asleep ;
If some small, trusting heart should break,
And hope become despair,
Don't let it be, I beg of you,
Because YOU didn't care !

THURSDAY—DECEMBER 21.

TIME marches on.

Eighty years or so ago, Mary Slessor left Dundee to take the Christian message to the people of Calabar.

With others then and ever since, she did wonderful work, spreading a light into the darkest places of Africa.

Why do I remind you of this?

Well, it happened that a coloured minister from Africa was in Scotland and he heard a Dundee church was making a special effort to bring the Christian message to people in its parish who had no church connection.

The minister volunteered to take part in the effort and that's why several Dundee families found a coloured minister on their doorstep, inviting them into the same fellowship which he had found in faraway Nyasaland.

What's stranger still is that the Dundee church which made this special effort was the very church in which Mary Slessor worshipped before she went as a missionary to Africa.

So now, by a strange turn of events, there was an African doing mission work in Dundee—thanks at least in part to the mission work which a Dundee lassie did in Africa many years ago.

FRIDAY—DECEMBER 22.

HEARD about the very small boy who always took a teddy-bear to bed with him?

One evening, just after prayers had been said, and Mum had tucked him in and given him a goodnight kiss, she whispered: " Often when I stand listening I hear you talking very quietly to Teddy. What do you tell him?"

" Well," replied the small boy, " after you've gone and the light is out, I hug Teddy, and I tell him all the happy, lovely, jolly things that have happened in the day."

" But don't you ever tell Teddy about your troubles?" asked Mum.

There was silence a minute. Then a rather sleepy little boy replied: " Well, Mummy, I always mean to tell Teddy my troubles . . . but there are such a lot of nice things to remember that I'm asleep before I reach the nasty ones."

SATURDAY—DECEMBER 23.

AS Christmas approaches, most of us find ourselves wondering why Christmas *has* to approach before we begin feeling kindly towards everybody, and ready to go to the trouble of taking them by happy surprise.

SUNDAY—DECEMBER 24.

AND, lo, the angel of the Lord came upon them, and the glory of the Lord shone round about them: and they were sore afraid. And the angel said unto them, Fear not: for, behold, I bring you good tidings of great joy, which shall be to all people. For unto you is born this day, in the city of David, a Saviour, which is Christ the Lord.

MONDAY—DECEMBER 25.

THIS seems an opportune moment to tell you about Jean, aged six, who last Christmas Day hurried off to show Granny her presents—and to take a wee surprise.

Arriving at Granny's, Jean was all excitement.

" Look, Granny," she said in her shrill voice, " I've brought you a present. I wrote the label myself, and I wrapped the ornament up in a bit of old newspaper. Mummy said it ought to have been wrapped in pretty coloured paper, but I forgot . . . and I told her you wouldn't mind because you'd know I'd put all my love inside !"

I leave this little tale with you—it has a message and meaning for Christmas, hasn't it? What does the price of your gift to somebody matter? The big thing is : Is your love inside?

TUESDAY—DECEMBER 26.

I MUST tell you about someone who has the spirit of Christmas not just on one day, but every day of the year. She is Mrs Nan Schonberg.

Many a young girl owes her chance of a decent life to Mrs Schonberg's helping hand, and children from drab homes bless her.

Many a fine she has paid to keep a man or a woman out of prison—though they never knew.

To many a poor soul she has taken food and clothes, tobacco and pocket money.

She also visits lonely folk in hospital, children in approved schools, and even prison, too.

Even when her mother—a wonderful woman who encouraged her daughter in her good works—died, Mrs Schonberg could still find time in her grief to smile and help others.

I'm proud to know such a great-hearted woman.

WEDNESDAY—DECEMBER 27.

ANOTHER year draws to its close—
Another milestone passed ;
And every Hogmanay must find
Us older than the last !
But sure we have more joys and smiles,
More blessings to recall,
More riches of the heart and mind—
We cannot count them all !
So, scorning doubt, despising fear,
We'll journey through the coming year !

THURSDAY—DECEMBER 28.

MRS SHORT thought she was in for flu.

But it was something far, far worse than she had ever dreaded. It was polio. And within 36 hours, Mrs Short, a young attractive mother of a little girl of five, was in an iron lung.

Her husband, Bill, was so stunned he scarcely remembers these first awful hours. But what did happen after that seems like a miracle.

Help appeared on every hand—from friends, from friends' friends and even complete strangers and, bit by bit, they began to build a new way of living for the stricken family.

Today, Mrs Short still lies in the machine without which she could not breathe. But, even so, she remains the centre of the family.

Every hour of the day, in an organised succession, helpers come to the house to be her hands and feet and do the things that she would do.

In all, nearly sixty people carry out this labour of love, making sure that between them Mrs Short is not alone and without help for a moment.

Truly, what a blessing are friends—especially when trouble comes to our door.

FRIDAY—DECEMBER 29.

HERE'S a lovely thought for tonight—or any night, for that matter.

Did you know that the opening chimes of Big Ben play a phrase from the accompaniment of Handel's wondrous aria—" I know that my Redeemer liveth "?

One man who knew and loved the voice of the bells often found himself humming in tune with them. Later, words began to fit the notes and before long he had composed a prayer set to the chimes.

It goes—" All through this hour, Lord, be my guide ; and by Thy power, no foot shall slide."

SATURDAY—DECEMBER 30.

NOT much left of the year, is there?

Isn't this a good excuse for doing something in secret?

Suppose you slip unnoticed into your bedroom, shut the door . . . and get down on your knees?

Why not kneel by the bed and say a prayer from the very bottom of your heart? Why not thank God for whatever mercies this old year has brought? Why not pray for forgiveness for your own shortcomings, and ask for strength and courage to do better in the days ahead?

Instead of carrying your own anxieties why not put all things into God's hands ?

It would take such a very few minutes . . . and you might rise to your feet feeling gloriously blessed, wonderfully empowered to go on into next year with confidence and faith and joy.

SUNDAY—DECEMBER 31.

GRACE be unto you, and peace, from God our Father, and from the Lord Jesus Christ.

Where The Photographs Were Taken

---

* *THE MESSAGE*—Waterville, Co. Kerry.

A HIGHLAND BURN—Inverie River, Knoydart, Inverness-shire.

TRACKS IN THE SNOW—Ben Dubhcraige, Perthshire.

AN OLD CASTLE—Barcaldine Castle, Argyll.

BREAKFAST—Royal Farm at Windsor.

MEMORY—Coire Garbhlach, Glen Feshie, Inverness-shire.

NOW DAY IS DONE—Gerrards Cross Common, Buckinghamshire.

TO A YOUNG PHOTOGRAPHER—Stourton, Wiltshire.

LIFE'S VOYAGE—Portloe, Cornwall.

A SUMMER DAY—Clachan, Argyll.

THE VIGIL—St. John's Kirk, Perth.

MORNING PAPERS—Cromarty.

THE WAY WE GO—Broughty Ferry, Angus.

PEACE—Hughenden, Buckinghamshire.

NEVER TOO OLD—Eynsford, Kent.

A SEASIDE VILLAGE—Southwold, Suffolk.

* By courtesy of the Irish Tourist Association.

Printed and Published in Great Britain by D. C. THOMSON & CO., LTD., and JOHN LENG & CO., LTD., London, Manchester and Dundee.